P · O · C · K · E · T · S

BUTTERFLIES
& MOTHS

POSTMAN BUTTERFLY

SWALLOWTAIL
BUTTERFLY
CATERPILLAR

OWL BUTTERFLY FEEDING

P·O·C·K·E·T·S

BUTTERFLIES & MOTHS

Written by
BARBARA TAYLOR

CINNABAR MOTH
LAYING EGGS

CHRYSALIS OF
QUEEN BUTTERFLY

ZEBRA BUTTERFLY

DK

A DK PUBLISHING BOOK

Project editor	Caroline Brooke
Art editor	Alexandra Brown
Senior editor	Hazel Egerton
Senior art editor	Jacquie Gulliver
Editorial consultant	David Carter
Picture research	Sharon Southren
Production	Josie Alabaster
US Editor	Constance M. Robinson
US Consultant	Eric Quinter, Department of Entomology, American Museum of Natural History

First American edition, 1996
2 4 6 8 10 9 7 5 3 1
Published in the United States by DK Publishing, Inc.,
95 Madison Avenue, New York, New York 10016

Library of Congress Cataloging-in-Publication Data
Taylor, Barbara, 1954–
  Butterflies and moths / by Barbara Taylor.
    p. cm. – (DK pockets)
  Includes index.
  Summary: Provides information on the behavior, appearance, habitats, and identification of butterflies and moths in all kinds of environments.
  ISBN 0-7894-0605-5
  1. Butterflies–Juvenile literature. 2. Moths–Juvenile literature.
  [1. Butterflies. 2. Moths.] I. Title. II. Series.
QL544.2.T38 1996   95–42177
595.78–dc20   CIP
                                                     AC

Color reproduction by Colourscan, Singapore
Printed and bound in Italy by L.E.G.O.

CONTENTS

How to use this book

These pages show you how to use *Pockets: Butterflies & Moths*. The book is divided into sections, each opening with a picture page. There is an introductory section at the beginning of the book and a reference section at the back. The central six sections look at butterflies and moths in different habitats.

HABITATS

The main section of the book is arranged into habitats. In each habitat section you will find information on the habitat, and examples of the types of moths and butterflies that live there.

CORNER CODING
Corners of the habitat pages are color-coded to remind you which habitat section you are in.

- TEMPERATE WOODLANDS
- TROPICAL RAIN FORESTS
- WETLANDS
- GRASSLANDS AND BARRENS
- DRY REGIONS AND CAVES
- ARCTIC AND MOUNTAINS

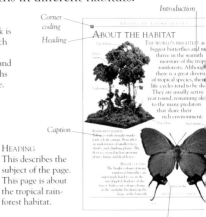

Introduction

Corner coding

Heading

ABOUT THE HABITAT

THE WORLD'S BRIGHTEST and biggest butterflies and moths thrive in the warmth and moisture of the tropical rainforests. Although there is a great diversity of tropical species, their life-cycles tend to be short. They are usually active year round, remaining alert to the many predators that share their rich environment.

Caption

RAINFOREST HABITAT
Tall trees with straight trunks form a leafy canopy. Beneath is an understory of smaller trees, shrubs, and climbing plants. The floor is covered in low-growing plants, fungi, and dead leaves.

BRIGHT COLORS
The bright colours of many rainforest butterflies are surprisingly hard to see in the sun-dappled shadows of the forest. Birds and others chasing the sunlight, breaking up the shape of the butterfly.

Annotation

HEADING
This describes the subject of the page. This page is about the tropical rain-forest habitat.

INTRODUCTION
This provides a clear, general overview of the subject. After reading the introduction, you should have an idea of what the pages are about.

CAPTIONS
AND ANNOTATIONS
Each illustration has a caption. Annotations, in *italics*, point out features of an illustration and usually have leader lines.

RUNNING HEADS
These remind you which section you are in. The left-hand page gives the section name. The right-hand page gives the subject. This "About the Habitat" page is in the Tropical Rain Forests section.

FACT BOXES
Many pages have fact boxes. These contain at-a-glance information about the subject. This fact box gives details such as the area of rain forest that is cut down every second.

REFERENCE SECTION
This section has yellow pages and appears at the back of the book. You will find useful facts, figures, and charts. These pages show which habitats and species are at risk.

Running head   *Fact box*

Label

GLOSSARY
At the back of the book is a glossary that explains the more complicated or technical words that appear in the text.

LABELS
For extra clarity, some pictures are accompanied by labels. These may provide extra information, or identify a picture when it is not immediately obvious from the text what it is.

INDEX
There are two indexes at the back of the book. The subject index lists every subject alphabetically. The common and scientific name index lists all the moths and butterflies that are in the book.

INTRODUCTION TO BUTTERFLIES AND MOTHS

BUTTERFLIES AND MOTHS

FOSSIL OF MOTH'S WING

FROM BRILLIANT blue Morpho butterflies to giant Atlas moths, these insects have an amazing variety of shapes, sizes, and colors. They can be distinguished from other insects by their long, hollow feeding tube (proboscis) and by the dustlike scales covering their wings and bodies.

DINOSAUR DAYS
Moths first appeared on Earth between 100 and 190 million years ago during the age of the dinosaurs. Butterflies came on the scene much later – about 40 million years ago. They probably evolved alongside flowering plants.

CLOSE-UP OF WING

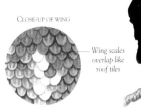

Wing scales overlap like roof tiles

LEPIDOPTERA FACTS

• Butterflies and moths belong to the insect order called *Lepidoptera*, meaning "scaly wings."

• There are about 170,000 known species of *Lepidoptera*. Only 10 percent are butterflies; the rest are moths.

• There may be 200 to 600 scales per square millimeter of wing.

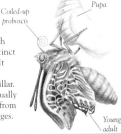

Pupa

Coiled-up proboscis

LIFE CYCLE
Each butterfly or moth goes through four distinct stages during its life. It starts as an egg that hatches into a caterpillar. The caterpillar eventually changes into a pupa, from which the adult emerges.

Young adult

PEACOCK BUTTERFLY

Long antenna
for feeling and
smelling
surroundings

Hairs on thorax
help keep
butterfly warm

Head with
large
compound eyes

Eyespot diverts
predators'
attention away
from body

Veins
strengthen
wings

ADULT FEATURES
Like all insects, adult butterflies and
moths have six legs and a hard external
skeleton to protect the body, which is
divided into three parts: head, thorax,
and abdomen. Most species also have
two pairs of wings, which are either
hooked or held together in flight.

1 3

Telling the difference

The division of *Lepidoptera* into butterflies and moths is an artificial one, based on a number of observable differences. Most butterflies fly by day and are brightly colored. Moths tend to be night fliers and have drab-colored wings, although some do fly by day and have bright colors. When resting, butterflies usually hold their wings upright, while moths spread out their wings or fold them flat over their bodies.

Threadlike antenna

BRINDLED BEAUTY MOTH

Strong, fat, hairy body helps to keep insect warm at night

Long, narrow wings

MOTH WINGS

There are many more moths than butterflies, and the colors, shapes, and sizes of moths' wings are much more varied. Moth wings tend to be longer and narrower than butterfly wings. At rest, moths often slide their forewings over their hind wings, making a triangular shape.

Dull camouflage colors on wings

BUTTERFLY WINGS
When butterflies
land to feed or
rest, they are
vulnerable to attack
from predators. A
typical butterfly shows
only the undersides of its
wings when it rests. The
undersides tend to be
patterned to camouflage
the resting butterfly.

*Intricate
pattern breaks
up shape of
butterfly*

*Underside
of wing*

*Feathery
antennae of
moth*

*Club on end of
butterfly's
antenna*

ANTENNAE
A good way to tell the
difference between a
butterfly and a moth is
to look at the antennae.
A butterfly antenna has
a club on the end;
moths have various types
of antennae, ranging
from single strands to
feathery branches.

HEDYLID MOTH

BUTTERFLY OR MOTH?
Hedylid "moths" from South
America are hard to categorize.
They are probably more closely
related to butterflies than to moths.
Although they have the antennae
of a moth, they have the flattened
body of a butterfly.

TYPES OF MOTHS

THERE IS AN incredible
variety in the size, color,
and shape of moths, from
the spectacular Emperor
moths and bright Burnets to
the small Micromoths and
dull-colored Owlet moths.
They are grouped into over
100 families. These pages
show just five examples of
the many families.

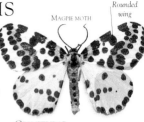

MAGPIE MOTH

Rounded wing

GEOMETRIDAE
Geometers have thin bodies, large,
rounded wings, and a weak,
fluttering flight. In some species,
the females are wingless. The
caterpillars "loop" across their food
plants, as if measuring them.

*Males often
have feathery
antennae*

SATURNIIDAE
This family is
made up of
the large and
magnificent
Emperor moths.
Many have
eyespots or
translucent patches
on their wings.
Adults have no
mouthparts and so
cannot feed. Their
cocoons may be used
to make coarse silk.

*Translucent
patches*

ORIZABA SILKMOTH

1 6

SPHINGIDAE

Commonly called Sphinx moths (or Hawkmoths), this family of moths has streamlined wings and strong bodies. Speedy fliers, some can fly up to 30 mph (50 kmh). Many such Hawkmoths hover like hummingbirds over deep-throated flowers. The large caterpillars usually have a pointed horn at the end of their bodies.

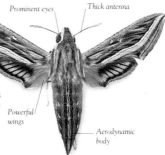

Prominent eyes

Thick antenna

Powerful wings

Aerodynamic body

SILVER-STRIPED HAWKMOTH

BROWN HOODED OWLET

Raised tufts on back of robust body

NOCTUIDAE

This is one of the largest moth families, with over 25,000 species. Most Noctuidae fly only at night, and for this reason are commonly known as Owlet moths. Some Noctuid caterpillars, such as Cutworms and Armyworms, are serious pests that attack crop plants.

ZYGAENIDAE

These small- to medium-sized moths are mainly day-fliers. They have bright colors or patterns to warn predators that they are poisonous. Most have well-developed tongues and their antennae are thickened toward the tip. The poisonous caterpillars are thick and sluglike.

FIERY CAMPYLOTES

Warning colors

TYPES OF BUTTERFLIES

ALTHOUGH BUTTERFLIES are remarkable for their bold and brilliant colors and beautiful shapes, there are fewer species of butterflies than there are species of moths. Butterflies are usually grouped into five families.

Large, robust body and head

BRAZILIAN SKIPPER

HESPERIIDAE
The butterflies of this family are commonly known as Skippers. Unlike other butterflies, they frequently lack clubbed antennae and, when resting, they fold their forewings over their backs.

Iridescent colors flash in sunlight

Eyespots and tails create a false head to confuse predators

PAPILIONIDAE
These large, colorful butterflies tend be powerful fliers. Many have "tails" their hind wings and are popularly known as Swallowtails. This family includes the tailless Birdwings, foun in tropical Australasia.

PAPILIO PALINURUS
SWALLOWTAIL

PIERIDAE

These butterflies are mostly white, yellow, or orange. Their bright colors come from waste products, which are deposited inside their scales. Though many species are tropical, they are found in all regions of the world and many migrate.

CABBAGE BUTTERFLY

Simple black wing markings

Body covered in hairlike white scales

SILVER-STUDDED BLUE

LYCAENIDAE

About 40 percent of all butterflies belong to this family of small, jewel-like butterflies. It includes the Blues, Coppers, and Hairstreaks. Males and females are often different colors, and the upperside of the wing is a brighter color than the underside.

White spots on forewing

NYMPHALIDAE

The distinguishing feature of this group is that the two front legs are small and cannot be used for walking. The family includes some of the most brilliant butterflies in the world, such as the Emperors, Monarchs, and Fritillaries. They are sometimes called "Brush-footed butterflies" after the thick tufts of scales on the front legs of the males.

PAINTED LADY

Scalloped hind wing

WINGS AND FLIGHT

MOTHS AND BUTTERFLIES FLY to escape predators, seek mates, and find food and places to live. Their wings are made of a thin, tough, transparent membrane supported by rigid veins. Flight patterns vary from the energetic darting of Skippers to the fluttering of Cabbage butterflies.

Prominent veins

SMALLER WOOD
NYMPH BUTTERFLY

WING VEINS
Butterfly and moth wings have veins that contain blood, air-carrying tubes, and nerves. They allow the delicate wings to twist, bend, and resist air pressure in flight. The pattern of veins differs from species to species.

JOINING THE WINGS
In butterflies and a few moths, a lobe on the hind wing overlaps and grips the forewing. Most moths have one or more bristles on the hind wing. These fit on the forewing behind a flap or catch.

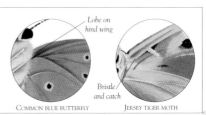

Lobe on hind wing

Bristle and catch

COMMON BLUE BUTTERFLY

JERSEY TIGER MOTH

OLEANDER
HAWKMOTH

FAST FLIERS
Resembling tiny jet planes when at rest, Hawkmoths zoom through the dusk on their powerful streamlined wings. Like other night-flying moths, they fly toward the lights of streets and houses, confused by their brightness. They are frequently found on or close to store windows.

*Long, narrow
forewing*

SILVER-WASHED
FRITILLARY

*Downward
flap*

*Gliding on a
current of air*

*Wings move
backward and
downward, pushing
butterfly forward*

BUTTERFLY FLIGHT
Most butterflies have a rather lazy "flap and glide" flight. Some butterflies, such as large-winged Swallowtails, are good gliders while others, such as these Fritillaries, can only glide short distances.

MOTHS WITHOUT WINGS
Some female moths, such as this Winter moth, have no wings (or only tiny wings) and cannot fly. Since they hatch in winter or early spring when the winds can be strong, they are less likely to be blown off course if they have no wings.

2 1

Color and scales

Wings are colored and patterned to
help moths and butterflies blend with
their surroundings, regulate their body
temperature, drive away predators, and
attract mates. The colors are formed
either by pigments contained in the
wing scales or by the way the structure
of the scales reflects the sunlight.
Chemicals produced by the butterfly or
moth are responsible for the pigments.

Moth shedding scales

SLIDING SCALES

Each time a butterfly or moth flaps
its wings, some of the powderlike
scales fall off. Often, the age of a
moth or butterfly can be
estimated by how many
scales have been lost.

ATLAS MOTH

LOOKING CLOSER

At close range, the rows
of overlapping scales are
visible to the naked eye.
Scales are flat, platelike hairs on
short stalks that fit into tiny pockets
on the wing membrane. Each scale
contains only one color. It is the
different concentration of pigment in
each scale that produces the variety of
colors on a wing.

Translucent patches

Powderlike scales

Pigmentary color

WINGS WITHOUT SCALES

Some butterflies and moths, such as the Esmeralda Butterfly or the Bumble Bee Sphinx Moth, have no scales on large areas of their wings. Since the scales fall off during the first flight, they are called deciduous scales. Many butterflies and moths with deciduous scales mimic bees and wasps.

ESMERALDA BUTTERFLY

Transparent, scaleless areas on wings

BRAZILIAN MORPHO WING

Metallic blue

SHIMMERING WINGS

The iridescent blue colors of this Morpho wing result from the way light is reflected or broken up by specially structured scales on the wing. These scales, which are arranged in layers, catch the light to produce different shades of blue.

Male disperses scent to attract female

SCHULZE'S AGRIUS BUTTERFLY

Androconia on hindwing

RELEASING SCENT

Some scales, called androconia, are modified for dispersing scent. They are usually long and slender with a tuft of fine hairs at the tip. Androconia are connected to scent glands in the wing membrane, and scent is released up through the hollow scales into the air.

SENSES

BUTTERFLIES AND MOTHS rely on their
senses for survival. Their bodies are covered
with sensory hairs that, according to the
position on the body, respond to
different sensations – smell,
taste, and touch. Butterflies
and moths have compound
eyes that are linked
to nerves inside
the body.

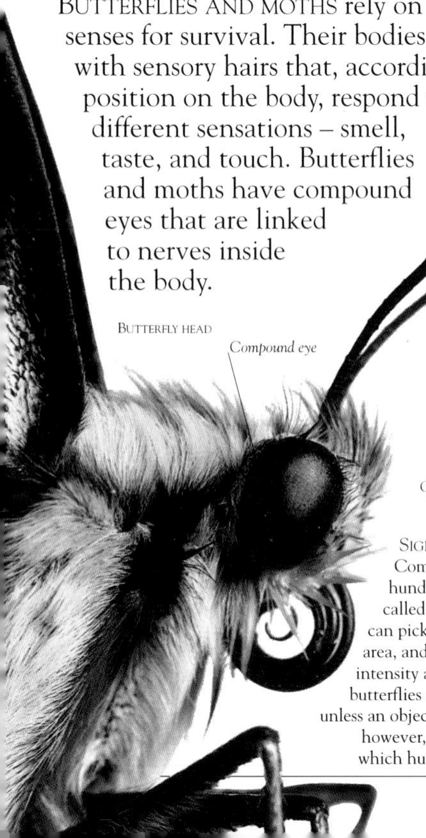

BUTTERFLY HEAD

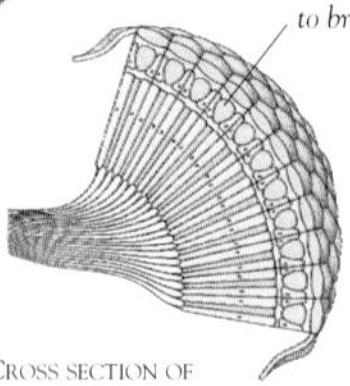

Compound eye

*Each ommatidium is
linked to a nerve
that sends messages
to brain*

CROSS SECTION OF
COMPOUND EYE

SIGHT
Compound eyes consist of
hundreds or thousands of lenses
called ommatidia. This type of eye
can pick up movement over a wide
area, and can also detect light
intensity and color. Moths and
butterflies cannot focus on details
unless an object is very close. They can,
however, detect ultraviolet light,
which humans cannot see.

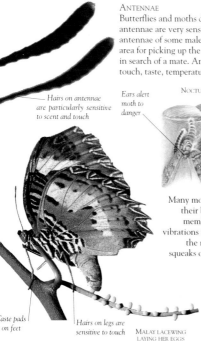

ANTENNAE

Butterflies and moths do not have noses, but their antennae are very sensitive to smells. The feathery antennae of some male moths have a larger surface area for picking up the odors given off by females in search of a mate. Antennae are sensitive to touch, taste, temperature, and wind movement.

Hairs on antennae are particularly sensitive to scent and touch

Ears alert moth to danger

NOCTUID MOTH

EARS

Many moths have ears on the sides of their bodies. These consist of thin membranes, which pick up sound vibrations from the air. At night, when the moths hear the high-pitched squeaks of bats, they dodge out of the way and avoid being eaten.

Taste pads on feet

Hairs on legs are sensitive to touch

MALAY LACEWING LAYING HER EGGS

TASTING WITH FEET

When a female butterfly is ready to lay her eggs, she uses the taste pads on her feet to find plants that the caterpillars can eat. Young caterpillars are too small to crawl far and need to find nourishment quickly or they will die.

SENSES FACTS

• Some moths have additional simple eyes (ocelli).

• A male Emperor moth can smell a female about 6 miles (11 km) away.

• The antennae of some moths are 5 times the length of their wings.

FEEDING AND DRINKING

MOST ADULT BUTTERFLIES AND MOTHS suck up liquid food through their strawlike proboscis. The most common food is sweet flower nectar, but some species feed on tree sap, rotting fruit, bird droppings, or moist manure, or from the fluid around the eyes of living animals. A few moths have jaws to chew flower pollen.

MORGAN'S
SPHINX

Uncoiled
proboscis
(feeding
tube)

Deep-throated
flower

PROBOSCIS
The length of the proboscis varies in different species to suit the flowers on which the insect feeds. The proboscis of the African Morgan's Sphinx moth is far longer than its body. It penetrates deep inside the flower to reach the hidden nectar.

INDIAN
MOON MOTH

Food stored
in body
sustains moth
throughout
adult life

STORING FOOD
Some moths, such as this Indian Moon Moth, do not feed at all as adults. They live off the energy in food stored in their bodies during the caterpillar stage. These moths either have a small proboscis or no proboscis at all.

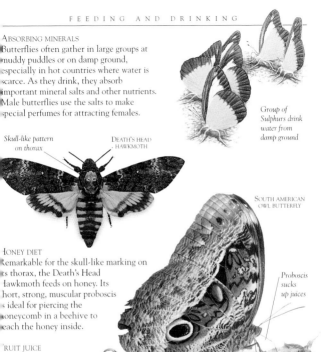

ABSORBING MINERALS

Butterflies often gather in large groups at muddy puddles or on damp ground, especially in hot countries where water is scarce. As they drink, they absorb important mineral salts and other nutrients. Male butterflies use the salts to make special perfumes for attracting females.

Group of Sulphurs drink water from damp ground

Skull-like pattern on thorax

DEATH'S HEAD HAWKMOTH

SOUTH AMERICAN OWL BUTTERFLY

HONEY DIET

Remarkable for the skull-like marking on its thorax, the Death's Head Hawkmoth feeds on honey. Its short, strong, muscular proboscis is ideal for piercing the honeycomb in a beehive to reach the honey inside.

FRUIT JUICE

Rotting fruit is a popular meal for many butterflies and moths, including these Owl butterflies. As the fruit rots, it breaks down into liquids. The butterfly tastes the juices with two mouthparts, called palps, at the base of its proboscis.

Proboscis sucks up juices

Palps

LIFE CYCLE

THERE ARE FOUR distinct stages in the life of a butterfl
or moth – egg, caterpillar, pupa, and adult. The whole
process of change is called complete metamorphosis.
The length of each phase depends on the species and
climate. A life cycle in the tropics might last about
three weeks, while in colder climates, it may last
several months or longer.

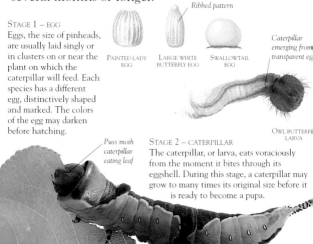

Ribbed pattern

PAINTED LADY
EGG

LARGE WHITE
BUTTERFLY EGG

SWALLOWTAIL
EGG

*Caterpillar
emerging from
transparent egg*

OWL BUTTERFL
LARVA

STAGE 1 – EGG
Eggs, the size of pinheads,
are usually laid singly or
in clusters on or near the
plant on which the
caterpillar will feed. Each
species has a different
egg, distinctively shaped
and marked. The colors
of the egg may darken
before hatching.

*Puss moth
caterpillar
eating leaf*

STAGE 2 – CATERPILLAR
The caterpillar, or larva, eats voraciously
from the moment it bites through its
eggshell. During this stage, a caterpillar may
grow to many times its original size before it
is ready to become a pupa.

STAGE 3 – PUPA

Within the hard, protective case of a pupa, the caterpillar is transformed into an adult. The pupa appears almost lifeless – it does not feed and rarely moves – but within the case there is plenty of activity. The body of the larva is liquefied and the cells are reorganized into the features of the adult.

CITRUS SWALLOWTAIL BUTTERFLY

Developing wing veins

Camouflaged leaflike chrysalis

COCOON OF OAK SILKMOTH

Leaves and silken threads protects the pupa

Dense web of silk

PROTECTING THE PUPA

Since the pupa cannot move, the insect is vulnerable to predators. The color and shape of a butterfly pupa, or chrysalis, are adapted to blend with a pupa's surroundings. Moth pupae are often further protected inside a cocoon of silk or plant debris, such as leaves and twigs.

COURTING PASSION-VINE BUTTERFLIES

STAGE 4 – ADULT

Soon after the butterfly or moth has broken through the pupal case, it flies off in search of a mate. A vital role of the adult is to mate and disperse its eggs to ensure the survival of its species. Adults do not grow, and if they feed, it is only to replace the energy they have used up by flying around.

Courtship and mating

When ready to mate, the adult butterfly or moth has to find a mate of the same species. Butterflies and moths must usually look, feel, and smell right to each other before mating can take place. They are attracted by the particular colors and patterns of their own species, and by scented chemical substances called pheromones. Butterflies and moths release these perfumed signals when they are ready to mate.

Feathery antenna of moth detects scent

SCENT TRAIL
Night-flying moths cannot use color to attract and recognize a mate. Instead, the male uses his sensitive antennae to pick up the perfumed trail of pheromones left by the female. Each species has a different scent.

Brightly coloured male

CRAMER'S BLUE MORPHOS

Larger wings of female

SEX DIFFERENCES
Male and female butterflies often have different colors, like these Central American butterflies. Males tend to be more colorful, but females are usually larger than males. Females seem to be attracted to males with wings that reflect ultraviolet light.

Female

Abdomens join together so male can fertilize female's eggs

Male claspers hold female's body

Male

SWALLOWTAILS

MATING
Both butterflies and moths mate end to end, with the male and female facing in opposite directions. Once they are joined, the pair may fly together, keeping out of sight of predators. Mating can last from 20 minutes to a few hours.

LAYING EGGS
After mating, the male flies off to find another female and the female searches for a plant on which to lay her eggs. She usually chooses the plant on which the caterpillar will feed, and sticks the eggs firmly to the plant with a secretion from her body. Species that feed on a wide range of plants may scatter eggs over them in flight.

Cinnabar moth laying eggs

Caterpillar growth

Many caterpillars, or larvae, hatch out of their eggs after about a week, but some remain in their shells for several months over winter. Caterpillars eat voraciously, growing quickly and building up energy supplies for use later in the life cycle. Unlike the adults, caterpillars do not have a liquid diet and use biting mouthparts, instead of a proboscis, to feed. Although caterpillars can strip a tree of all its leaves, they are very particular about the plants they will eat. If no suitable plant is available, caterpillars will starve to death rather than eat anything else.

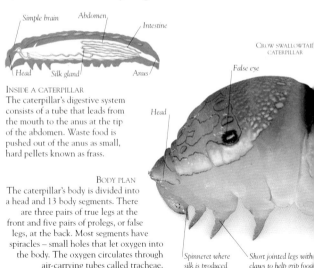

Simple brain   *Abdomen*   *Intestine*

Head   *Silk gland*   *Anus*

CROW SWALLOWTAIL CATERPILLAR

False eye

Head

INSIDE A CATERPILLAR
The caterpillar's digestive system consists of a tube that leads from the mouth to the anus at the tip of the abdomen. Waste food is pushed out of the anus as small, hard pellets known as frass.

BODY PLAN
The caterpillar's body is divided into a head and 13 body segments. There are three pairs of true legs at the front and five pairs of prolegs, or false legs, at the back. Most segments have spiracles – small holes that let oxygen into the body. The oxygen circulates through air-carrying tubes called tracheae.

Spinneret where silk is produced   *Short jointed legs with claws to help grip food*

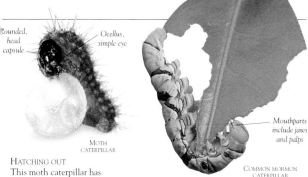

Rounded, head capsule

Ocellus, simple eye

MOTH CATERPILLAR

HATCHING OUT
This moth caterpillar has bitten its way out of the egg. Eating the eggshell gives the growing caterpillar the nutrients it needs.

Mouthparts include jaws and palps

COMMON MORMON CATERPILLAR

FEEDING
Caterpillars bite off pieces of leaf with their powerful mandibles (jaws). Sensory organs, called palps, are used to taste the food to ensure that it is suitable to eat, and the mandibles shred it into pieces.

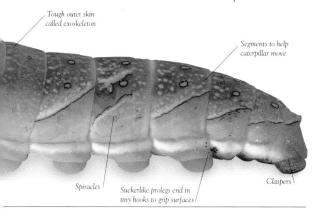

Tough outer skin called exoskeleton

Segments to help caterpillar move

Spiracles

Suckerlike prolegs end in tiny hooks to grip surfaces

Claspers

Developing and moving

The tough, flexible covering on the outside of a caterpillar's body allows it to wriggle and crawl, but will not stretch enough for it to grow. Every so often, the caterpillar has to molt, or shed its old skin. This process, called ecdysis, usually happens four or five times during a caterpillar's life. While molting, larvae often spin silken pads to fix themselves to plants. Unlike the adults, caterpillars can produce silk.

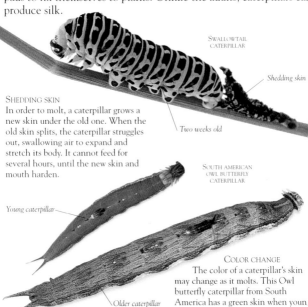

SWALLOWTAIL
CATERPILLAR

Shedding skin

SHEDDING SKIN

In order to molt, a caterpillar grows a new skin under the old one. When the old skin splits, the caterpillar struggles out, swallowing air to expand and stretch its body. It cannot feed for several hours, until the new skin and mouth harden.

Two weeks old

SOUTH AMERICAN
OWL BUTTERFLY
CATERPILLAR

Young caterpillar

COLOR CHANGE

The color of a caterpillar's skin may change as it molts. This Owl butterfly caterpillar from South America has a green skin when young and a brown skin when it is older.

Older caterpillar ready to pupate

Dangling from strong thread of silk

SILKEN LIFELINE
Many caterpillars, such as this Oak Leaf Roller caterpillar, use a silken line to escape predators. They drop from a branch or a leaf, holding tightly to the end of the silk and may spin around so fast that they become almost invisible. When the danger has passed, the caterpillars climb up the silk and start feeding again.

OAK LEAF ROLLER CATERPILLAR

Silk protects pupa

OAK SILKMOTH CATERPILLAR

SPINNING SILK
Moth caterpillars often spin a silken cocoon to protect their pupae. Caterpillars produce silk from a gland in the body, and the silk threads are drawn out by spinnerets under the head. The silk is liquid at first, but soon hardens when it meets the air.

Pulls up back legs so body loops

Extends front legs forward

LOOPER CATERPILLAR
Caterpillars of the moth family Geometridae have fewer prolegs than other caterpillars, and the middle part of the body has no legs at all. They are often called Looper caterpillars or Inchworms because of the way they move. The caterpillars appear to advance inch by inch by repeatedly arching their bodies into a loop.

Stretches body out flat

Caterpillar to adult

When a caterpillar is fully grown, it finds a suitable place to change into a pupa (pupate) and then sheds its skin for the last time. Inside the protective case of the pupa, an amazing transformation takes place. All the parts of the caterpillar's body are chemically broken down into their various components, which then develop to make the body and wings of the adult. Some of the changes can be seen through the pupal skin. The time it takes to change into an adult varies from weeks to months, depending on the climate and species.

CHANGE
The larva of this Swallowtail butterfly is preparing to pupate. It spins a silken loop for support and hangs from a stem. Soon, its skin will split along the back, revealing the green pupa inside.

BUILDING BODIES
The pupa darkens and hardens on contact with the air to protect the developing butterfly. All parts of the adult body begin to take shape. The pupa can be either green or brown to match its surroundings.

BUTTERFLY PUPA, OR CHRYSALIS

Silk loop, or safety belt

Wings and head

Abdomen developing

Hook at end of Sphinx moth pupa

UNDERGROUND PUPA
Some moths, such as this Sphinx moth, pupate underground, where they are safer from predators. The caterpillar hollows out a chamber and binds the walls with saliva and strands of silk.

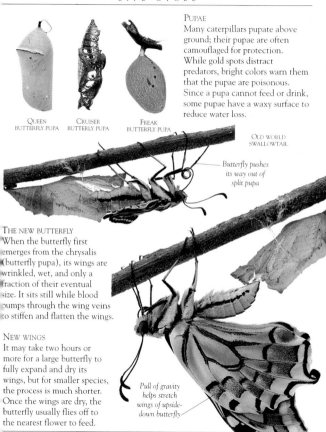

PUPAE

Many caterpillars pupate above ground; their pupae are often camouflaged for protection. While gold spots distract predators, bright colors warn them that the pupae are poisonous. Since a pupa cannot feed or drink, some pupae have a waxy surface to reduce water loss.

QUEEN
BUTTERFLY PUPA

CRUISER
BUTTERFLY PUPA

FREAK
BUTTERFLY PUPA

OLD WORLD
SWALLOWTAIL

*Butterfly pushes
its way out of
split pupa*

THE NEW BUTTERFLY

When the butterfly first emerges from the chrysalis (butterfly pupa), its wings are wrinkled, wet, and only a fraction of their eventual size. It sits still while blood pumps through the wing veins to stiffen and flatten the wings.

NEW WINGS

It may take two hours or more for a large butterfly to fully expand and dry its wings, but for smaller species, the process is much shorter. Once the wings are dry, the butterfly usually flies off to the nearest flower to feed.

*Pull of gravity
helps stretch
wings of upside-
down butterfly*

SURVIVAL

WITHOUT SHARP TEETH, claws, or stings to defend themselves, moths and butterflies rely on more subtle means of protection. These range from camouflage to bright colors that warn predators they are poisonous. Caterpillars may have sharp spines or irritating hairs, or mimic harmful creatures and inedible objects.

Common Blue butterfly being eaten by spider

PREDATORS
Often attacked by birds and spiders, moths and butterflies are also threatened by small mammals and lizards. Moths that fly at night to avoid birds may be eaten by bats instead.

FALSE EYES
Eyespots on the wings fool predators into thinking that the head is on the wings. A butterfly or moth can still fly with parts of its wings missing, but an injury to the head or body is usually fatal.

Eyespots on edge of wings – far away from body

PAPILIO
PALINURUS
SWALLOWTAIL

INSECT DISGUISE
When the caterpillar of the
Lobster Moth is threatened, it
lifts up its head and scorpion-
like tail to make itself look
fierce. Young Lobster Moth
caterpillars resemble red
ants and often gather
together on branches.

LOBSTER MOTH
CATERPILLAR

Legs
grip leaf

RED UNDERWING MOTH

Spreading
wings to flash
red band

SHOCK TACTICS
Some moths and butterflies have
bright patches of color or false eyes
hidden away on their hind wings.
If danger threatens, they quickly
spread their wings and flash
their colors or eyespots to startle
an attacker.

Sharp
spikes

False
antenna

ZEBRA
CATERPILLAR

CATERPILLAR WEAPONS
The Zebra caterpillar becomes poisonous through
eating poisonous plants. It also has sharp spines to
protect its soft body. Other caterpillars have irritating
or poisonous hairs. A few caterpillars look like small
snakes – they have large, false eyes and shake their
heads vigorously from side to side when threatened.

Camouflage

Many butterflies and moths use camouflage to defend themselves from predators. Some species resemble inanimate objects such as twigs or dead leaves; others may be colored to match their backgrounds, or they may have patterns on their wings that help break up their body shape. Camouflage is used as a survival technique throughout the life cycle and is most effective when the insect keeps still.

PEPPERED MOTH CATERPILLAR

Scars and bud-like markings

Larvae of tropical Swallowtail butterflies

Larvae mimicking bird droppings

TWIG MIMIC
This caterpillar rests at an angle, projecting itself from the main twig. When resting, the caterpillar is difficult to detect, since it mimics the color, texture, and shape of the twig. But any movement to find food makes it visible.

Tip pointed like a leaf

CHRYSALIS

INEDIBLE
By mimicking bird droppings, these caterpillars trick birds into leaving them alone. Some larvae, such as Japanese Swallowtail caterpillars, start out by looking like bird droppings but, as they grow larger, they adapt their disguise to their increased size. Japanese Swallowtail larvae eventually resemble small snakes.

LEAFLIKE
The chrysalis of the Cloudless Giant Sulphur butterfly is the same shape and color as a green leaf, blending in with its leafy habitats in North and Central America. Since pupae are unable to move, camouflage is their best means of defense.

Speckled form

PEPPERED MOTH

Black form is common in polluted areas

ENVIRONMENTAL CHANGE
Night-flying moths that rest by day are often especially well camouflaged. In some industrial areas, speckled Peppered Moths have been replaced by darker-colored Peppered Moths. These blend more effectively with tree trunks darkened by pollution.

Spots like those on decaying leaves

LEAF BUTTERFLY
A number of caterpillars, pupae, and adults mimic dry, dead, curled-up leaves. A few butterflies, such as this Indian Leaf Butterfly, are remarkable for their similarity to flattened leaves. The wings are shaped like leaves, with pointed tips to resemble stems, and there are lines on the undersides that look like the veins of a leaf.

Dark line mimicking midrib of leaf

INDIAN LEAF BUTTERFLY

Warning colors and mimicry

Some moths and butterflies are brightly
colored to warn predators that they
are poisonous. Others confuse
predators by mimicking harmful
creatures. Some harmless butterflies
mimic the warning colors of poisonous
species; common warning colors are red,
orange, yellow, and black. In some
species, only the females are mimics,
since they need extra protection if they
are to survive and lay eggs.

Eating
poisonous
milkweed

Stripes of
warning color

EATING POISONS
Some caterpillars, such as
Monarch larvae, become
poisonous from eating
toxic plants. They store
the poisons in
their body.

MONARCH BUTTERFLY

Warning colors

MIMIC
When a harmless
butterfly mimics a
poisonous one, it
is called Batesian
mimicry, after the
nineteenth-century
British naturalist H. W. Bates.
The edible Viceroy butterfly
shares the bright orange and black
warning colors of the Monarch. Predators,
unable to tell them apart, usually leave both alone.

Foul-tasting,
leathery body

Adult contains
poisons eaten by
caterpillar

POSTMAN BUTTERFLY MIMICS

When two poisonous species look
similar, it is called Müllerian mimicry. Fritz
Müller, a German-born Brazilian biologist,
discovered the phenomenon in the
nineteenth century. These two
species of Postman butterflies share
the same warning colors as well
as similar habitats in Central and
South America. Predators soon
learn to avoid all species with
the same "uniform."

Postman look-alike

Form and warning colors common to many species

POSTMAN BUTTERFLY

SMALL POSTMAN

HORNET MOTH

Yellow head

WASP OR MOTH?

This Hornet Moth has transparent
wings and a body ringed in yellow and
black like a hornet (a species of large wasp).
Other harmless moths also look like bees or
wasps and even behave in a similar way.
They fly rapidly in bright sunshine, visit
flowers, and some even buzz as they fly.
Predators avoid them for fear of being stung.

Only the borders of the wings are covered with scales

Black and yellow warning colors

Migration and hibernation

Some butterflies and moths migrate in order to avoid bad weather or overcrowding, or to find a new place to live if their original habitat has been destroyed. They usually migrate in only one direction, from their place of birth to a new area. They may breed en route. Some species survive extreme weather by resting for long periods. This is called hibernation in cold weather and estivation during hot, dry spells.

Monarchs pass winter clinging to pine trees

Well-monitored migration routes over America

MONARCH BUTTERFLIES
Every autumn, large groups of Monarchs swarm across North America to hibernate in the mountain forests of southern California or Mexico. In spring, they (or their offspring) return northward alone or in small groups.

PAINTED LADIES
To avoid overcrowding, each spring millions of Painted Ladies follow a variety of migration routes throughout the world. They travel widely but in only one direction, crossing high mountain barriers and breeding en route.

When Painted Ladies travel north from the deserts of Africa, they cross the Alps

PAINTED LADY BUTTERFLY

In summer, these Hawkmoths look through the Pyrenean passes

HUMMINGBIRD HAWKMOTHS

These moths are strong fliers, regularly traveling long distances. In spring, they begin their flight from southern Europe to northern Europe, moving northward as the weather becomes warmer.

HUMMINGBIRD
HAWK-MOTH

ESTIVATION

During hot, dry weather, Bogong moths estivate in rock crevices and caves in the Australian Alps. When it gets cooler, they emerge from their dormant state. They fly, in large numbers, northward to low, cultivated land.

Bogong moths fly north when the weather is cooler

BOGONG MOTH

Peacock butterflies hanging

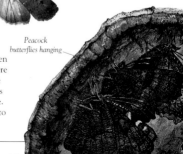

HIBERNATION

In temperate regions, butterflies and moths hibernate during the winter when it is too cold for them to move and there are few plants on which to feed. While some species hibernate as adults, others hibernate as eggs, caterpillars, or pupae. At rest, their life processes slow down to conserve energy. They reemerge when the weather is warmer.

FRIENDS AND FOES

ALTHOUGH SOME BUTTERFLIES
and moths are serious
pests, the vast majority
are harmless insects that
benefit the environment
by pollinating flowers.
Some species of caterpillars
feed on weeds, and others
have been cultivated for
centuries for their fine silk,
which is sold commercially.

*Silkmoths emerging
from silken cocoons*

SILK PRODUCERS

Silkworms (Silkmoth larvae) spin
fine silken threads for their
cocoons. They are bred on special
farms, where they are fed mulberry
leaves. The thread of one caterpill
can be as long as 2,625 ft (800 m).

*Proboscis
covered with
pollen*

*Butterfly carries
pollen from
flower to flower*

POLLINATION

Flowers have
nectar and
scent to
encourage visits
from butterflies and
moths. As they drink
nectar, dustlike grains of
pollen may stick to their
bodies. If they feed on
another flower of the same
kind, the male sex cells in the
pollen they carry may fertilize the
female sex cells. The plant can then
make seeds and reproduce.

CLOTHES MOTHS
The small, white caterpillars of
the Common Clothes Moth feed
on natural materials, such as
wool and fur. The False Clothes
Moth, or House Moth, attacks
natural and synthetic fibers like
nylon and polystyrene.

*Destructive pine
Emperor moth*

*Common Clothes
Moth eating felt*

FOREST PESTS
This caterpillar of the Pine
Emperor moth of South Africa
can strip pine trees of their
leaves, destroying large areas
of conifer plantation. In
Europe, conifer pests
include the larvae of the
Pine Processionary
moth and the Pine
Beauty moth.

PINE EMPEROR
MOTH
CATERPILLAR

Distinctive stripes

LARGE WHITE
CATERPILLARS

CABBAGE WHITES
The caterpillars of
the Large and the
Small White butterflies
devour cabbage
leaves, rapidly
reducing them to
skeletons. The Large
Whites feed on the outer
leaves, while the Small
Whites eat away at the
heart of the cabbage.

*Eating
cabbage leaf*

ENVIRONMENTAL CHANGE

BUTTERFLIES AND MOTHS
are particularly sensitive
to environmental change.
If nature's balance is
altered, an individual
species can become rare
or extinct. The variety
of species is threatened
by habitat change, by the
spread of farmland and
urban areas, by pest
control programs,
and by pollution.

QUEEN ALEXANDRA'S
BIRDWING

Brightly
colored
male

This
butterfly
legally
protected

HABITAT DESTRUCTION
This rare species is threatened by the
destruction of its rain-forest home in Papua
New Guinea. Rain forests throughout the
world are being destroyed at an alarming
rate since they are a source of timber,
farmland, and underground minerals.

PREDATORS

Recently, the number of Luna moths in northeastern America and southern Canada has declined. The electric lights of these heavily urbanized areas attract Luna moths, where they remain until they die or are eaten by predators. They have also been eaten by parasitic insects that have been introduced to these regions to control outbreaks of Gypsy moth pests.

LUNA MOTH

Scarce in Canada

HOMERUS SWALLOWTAIL

Appealing colors

Bands of yellow

COLLECTORS

The Homerus Swallowtail is found only in Jamaica. It is now a protected species, which means that it is illegal to collect it. Collecting affects populations of insects that are on the verge of extinction.

HABITATS AND SPECIES

• Large Copper and Large Blue butterflies were formerly extinct in Britain but have recently been reintroduced.

• The Apollo butterfly used to be common in the European Alps but is now a legally protected species.

• Habitats can be lost through building, plowing, overgrazing, draining wetlands, and cutting down forests.

HABITATS

THE GREATEST VARIETY of butterflies and moths is found in the shelter of tropical rain forests. The warm, humid climate provides a range of food sources. However, butterflies and moths survive in nearly all habitats from hot, dry deserts to frozen Arctic tundra. Many species live in more than one habitat.

NORTH AMERICA

SOUTH AMERICA

TEMPERATE WOODLANDS
Butterflies and moths prefer sunny clearings in broad-leaved or coniferous woodlands, where there are plenty of flowers on which they can feed. They survive the cold winter season by hibernating.

RAIN FORESTS
The rich plant growth in these hot, wet habitats encourages a remarkable diversity of exotic butterflies and moths.

ARCTIC AND MOUNTAINS
Only the hardiest of species can
live at high altitudes or survive the
extreme cold and winds of Arctic
tundra. However, mountain
meadows and forests provide
shelter and food plants.

DRY REGIONS AND CAVES
Few moths and butterflies are
attracted to the inhospitable
habitats created by low rainfall.
Caves provide a useful refuge
during very hot or cold weather.

GRASSLANDS AND BARRENS
From coastal lowlands to
tropical savanna, these habitats
provide a variety of grasses and
wildflowers to attract moths
and butterflies. However, there
is little shelter from winds and
bad weather.

WETLANDS
The waterlogged soils near
seas, rivers, and lakes provide a
range of food plants suitable for
some moths and butterflies.

TEMPERATE WOODLANDS

ABOUT THE HABITAT

TEMPERATE WOODLANDS have plenty of food plants and egg-laying sites to attract butterflies and moths. Some species are restricted to one type of woodland and many caterpillars can eat only certain woodland plants. Butterflies and moths favor sunny forest lanes and clearings rich in wild flowers.

WOODLAND LAYERS
Most butterflies and moths fly back and forth between the various layers of woodland to feed, seek a mate, or escape a predator.

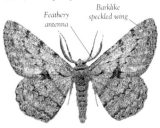

Feathery antenna

Barklike speckled wing

GREAT OAK
BEAUTY MOTH

SPECKLED WOOD
BUTTERFLY

Eyespots

CAMOUFLAGE
Many woodland butterflies and moths are camouflaged to look like bark or leaves. The colors of the Great Oak Beauty moth blend with the different tree trunks on which it rests. The caterpillars mimic twigs.

TERRITORIAL PATCH
A pair of Speckled Wood butterflies may be seen spiraling upward in a sunny woodland clearing. The male butterfly is defending his territory, using his eyespots to startle intruders. He courts females that enter his territorial patch.

LEOPARD MOTH

Boldly spotted wings

Six spots on thorax

Yellow spotting

SLOW START
The Leopard Moth is a caterpillar for two to three years. It eats into the hard wood of broad-leaved trees, digesting and absorbing nutrients slowly.

WOODLAND FACTS

• Many deciduous woods have been replaced by fast-growing conifer woods.

• Purple Emperors live in treetop colonies.

• Some caterpillars can strip trees of their leaves.

SEASONAL SURVIVAL
The Holly Blue butterfly survives the winter season as a chrysalis. The adults emerge in early spring and fly among the trees. They breed on shrubs.

HOLLY BLUE

DISGUISED
Young Tiger Swallowtail caterpillars look like fresh bird droppings. They feed on the leaves of willow and ash trees in Canada and the US.

TIGER SWALLOWTAIL

Tigerlike stripes

Hind wing tail

HEATH FRITILLARY

ON THE MOVE
Heath Fritillaries can only survive in clearings of freshly cut woodland. Every few years they move to newly felled areas. The search becomes harder as woods are replaced by farms and buildings.

Orange and brown pattern

CONIFER FORESTS

ONLY HARDY SPECIES OF butterflies and moths can survive the cold climate of conifer forests, which grow primarily in northern temperate regions. Many of the trees, such as fir, spruce, and pine, are evergreen and have needle-like leaves that are able to withstand the long, cold winters.

Black markings

PINE WHITE

PINE PROCESSIONARY MOTH

Prominent veins

PINE PEST
High among fir and pine trees, adult Pine White butterflies flutter weakly. They may descend to the forest floor to feed in the early morning or late afternoon. Their striped caterpillars look like pine needles and can be very destructive to pine woods.

FOLLOWING A THREAD
During the day, Pine Processionary moth larvae rest together in silken webs. At night, they set off in a long line to look for food. The head caterpillar spins a silken thread for the others to follow. Each caterpillar branches off to eat but returns to its nest guided by a thread of silk.

Procession of caterpillars

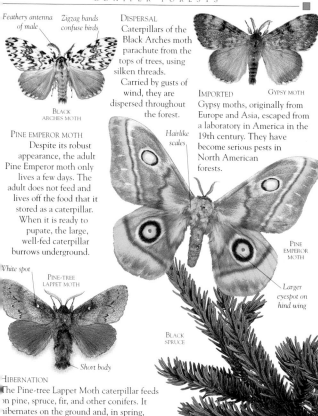

Feathery antenna of male

Zigzag bands confuse birds

BLACK ARCHES MOTH

DISPERSAL
Caterpillars of the Black Arches moth parachute from the tops of trees, using silken threads. Carried by gusts of wind, they are dispersed throughout the forest.

GYPSY MOTH

IMPORTED
Gypsy moths, originally from Europe and Asia, escaped from a laboratory in America in the 19th century. They have become serious pests in North American forests.

PINE EMPEROR MOTH
Despite its robust appearance, the adult Pine Emperor moth only lives a few days. The adult does not feed and lives off the food that it stored as a caterpillar. When it is ready to pupate, the large, well-fed caterpillar burrows underground.

Hairlike scales

PINE EMPEROR MOTH

Larger eyespot on hind wing

White spot

PINE-TREE LAPPET MOTH

Short body

BLACK SPRUCE

HIBERNATION
The Pine-tree Lappet Moth caterpillar feeds on pine, spruce, fir, and other conifers. It hibernates on the ground and, in spring, completes its development in the treetops.

EUCALYPTUS WOODLANDS

IN SOUTHEASTERN and southwestern Australia, butterflies and moths thrive among eucalyptus trees and flowering shrubs. Many of the species are unique to Australia.

Metallic blue scales

Eyespots

Ta

ANT SERVANTS
The caterpillars of the beautiful Common Imperial Blue live in groups and feed on species of wattle. Black ants feed on the sugary substances that the caterpillars secrete.

BAT MOTH
Female Giant Anthelids are the size of small bats, with a wingspan of up to 6 ¼ in (16 cm). The large, bristly caterpillars eat eucalyptus leaves and store up food in their bodies for use later in the life cycle.

Blackish brown forewings

GIANT
ANTHELID

Wavy yellow-orange line

Curved edge

CAMOUFLAGE
The bluish green caterpillar of the Emperor Gum Moth is well camouflaged among the eucalyptus leaves on which it feeds. Its oval cocoon, spun from silk and bark, hangs disguised on eucalyptus trunks.

THE EMPEROR
GUM MOTH

Well-developed eyespot to deter predator

AUSTRALIAN SKIPPER

The Eastern Flat Skipper is widely distributed in Australia. It flies early in the morning or at dusk, unless disturbed. During the day, it settles on the underside of leaves. The caterpillars live inside tents made from leaves.

Translucent spots

EASTERN FLAT SKIPPER

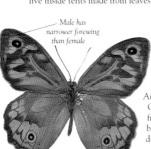

Male has narrower forewing than female

COMMON BROWN

DIFFERENCES

Found in southwest and southeast Australia, the wet season generation of Common Browns may be a different color from the dry season brood. The female butterflies are larger, and the sexes have different markings on their wings.

Only males have blue washes on each wing

WATTLE

Yellow spot

YELLOW-SPOT BLUE

YELLOW SPOT

Named after the yellow spots on the forewings, the Yellow-spot Blue lives only in wooded country in Australia. The green caterpillar hides by day under leaves on the ground and is attended by small, black ants. It emerges at night to feed on *Pimelea* leaves.

NORTHERN BROADLEAF

BUTTERFLIES OFTEN FLY in the treetops, but moths rarely leave the understoreys of these damp woods found in Asia, Europe, and North America. Broad-leaved trees, such as oak and birch, shed their leaves in autumn.

Thick, black margin on male

CALIFORNIA DOG-FACE
As it flits through the open woodlands, the California Dog-face butterfly is sometimes known as the "Flying Pansy." It is the state butterfly for California.

ROYAL WALNUT MOTH

Orange veins

Also known as Regal Moth

HORNED DEVILS
This beautiful North American moth pupates underground. Its horned caterpillars are called "Hickory Horned Devils" and feed on various trees including hickory and walnut.

MOURNING CLOAK

Maroon expanse

Golden border

MOURNING CLOAK
This butterfly is called the Mourning Cloak because of its somber colors. The adult hibernates but may sometimes fly on warm, winter days. It emits an audible "click" if a predator comes near.

hiny purple patch

Female has brown wings

PURPLE HAIRSTREAK

mall tail

HIGH FLIERS
Purple Hairstreaks keep mainly to the canopy and rarely descend to the ground. The adults feed on the sweet honeydew that aphids secrete over the tree tops. The caterpillars feed on the flower buds and leaves of oak trees.

Eyespot

DISAPPEARING WINGS
When resting on tree trunks, the Woodland Grayling butterfly usually closes its wings. It reveals the barklike pattern on the undersides of its hind wings. The caterpillars hibernate in chambers created out of fallen leaves.

WOODLAND GRAYLING

White band

Scalloped hind wing

White spot

POPLAR HAWKMOTH

DEAD-LEAF MOTH
At rest, the Poplar Hawkmoth resembles a bunch of dead leaves. If it is disturbed, it flashes the red patches on its wings to startle birds. Caterpillars feed on poplar, willow, alder, and birch trees. They pupate in the soil around the roots of trees.

Scalloped ing border

Red-brown patch

WOODLAND CLEARINGS

THE GREATEST VARIETY of
woodland butterflies and
moths is found in grassy
open areas such as woodland
paths and clearings. While
butterflies often bask in
the sun, moths usually
hide in the undergrowth.

*Soft, velvet
uppersides*

RINGLET

*Ring
eyespo*

GRASS EATERS

Ringlets flutter amongst the tall,
lush grasses of damp, sunny
clearings. They are among the
few butterflies that can fly in
light rain. The larvae can eat
only certain grasses.

ON PATROL

The delicate Wood White lives
in colonies. Males slowly patrol
paths and clearings in search of a
mate. Although females fly less,
they flit from flower to flower
drinking nectar.

WOOD WHITE

*Male Wood
Whites often
gather on puddles*

*Delicate
black
shading*

WHITE ADMIRALS

These butterflies prefer the
shade, gliding swiftly through
woodland openings. The females
retreat into the forest to lay their
glassy, green eggs on the leaves of
honeysuckle, the caterpillar's food plant.

WHITE
ADMIRAL

*Whit
band*

WINTER SLEEP
Adult Large Tortoiseshells
overwinter (hibernate) in
hollow trees or other sheltered
locations. Their long, hairy
scales help to keep them warm.
In spring, they emerge and
sunbathe with their wings held
wide open. The caterpillars live in
large silken webs on trees.

Hairs on thorax

Narrow forewing

COMMON
GLIDER

White streak

LARGE
TORTOISESHELL

Scalloped hind wing

Black-and-white bands on hind wing

GLIDING FLIGHT
The black-and-
white bands on the wings of the
Common Glider help to camouflage the
butterfly in the dappled sunlight of open
woodland. Its name describes the way it flies –
little flits are followed by long glides.

DUKE OF BURGUNDY
FRITILLARY

Orange spots on wing edge

ON GUARD
Duke of Burgundy Fritillaries live
in small colonies. The males defend
their territory against rivals, perhaps
perched on a blade of grass in a new
clearing. The females lay their eggs
on the undersides of marsh
marigold and primrose leaves.

Brown dots

FRITILLARIES AND CHECKERSPOTS

SPECKLED BUTTERFLIES often fly along forest margins, camouflaged by the dappled sunlight. They may roost in the treetops at night, descending to the woodland floor during the day to feed on bramble or thistle flowers. They appear to have only four legs, since the hairy front legs are too short to be used for walking.

Black bands on wing margins

CARDINAL

SUN TRAP
The Cardinal often basks in sunny clearings in southern Europe, North Africa, Iran, and Pakistan, holding its wings at a 45° angle. The beautiful rosy red patch on the underside of its forewings distinguishes it from many other Fritillaries.

Angular forewing   *Prominent clubbed antenna*

APHRODITE

VIOLET DIET
Female North American Aphrodite butterflies usually lay their eggs directly onto violet leaves in broadleaf and conifer woods. After hatching, the caterpillars hibernate and emerge the following spring. Like many other Fritillary larvae, they feed at night on the leaves of woodland violets.

Black spots on hindwing

Pale underside

DOTTED CHECKERSPOT FEMALE

Males are smaller than females

Checkered black-and-orange pattern

DOTTED CHECKERSPOT MALE

WING PATTERNS
The Dotted Checkerspot from North America has the black, orange, and yellow markings. These speckles help to conceal the butterflies in dappled sunlit woods. The undersides of the wings are much paler than the uppersides. The orange caterpillars are protected by orange and black spines.

Stripes of scent scales

Robust furry palps

WASH OF SILVER
Male Silver-washed Fritillaries have black bars on the veins of the forewings, which carry scent scales. The name of this butterfly comes from the wash of silver on the undersides of the hindwings. Silver-washed Fritillaries are unusual in laying their eggs on the bark of trees, such as oaks, near patches of violets.

Wing has scalloped edge

SILVER-WASHED FRITILLARY

TROPICAL RAIN FORESTS

ABOUT THE HABITAT

THE WORLD'S BRIGHTEST and biggest butterflies and moths thrive in the warmth and moisture of the tropical rain forests. Although there is a great diversity of tropical species, their life cycles tend to be short. They are usually active all year round, remaining alert to the many predators that share their rich environment.

Emergent trees

Forest canopy

Understory

Forest floor

Black margin

RAIN-FOREST HABITAT
Tall trees with straight trunks form a leafy canopy. Beneath is an understory of smaller trees, shrubs, and climbing plants. The floor is covered with low-growing plants, fungi, and dead leaves.

BRIGHT COLORS
The bright colors of many rain-forest butterflies are surprisingly hard to see in the sun-dappled shadows of the forest. Iridescent colors change in the sunlight, breaking up the shape of the butterfly.

Iridescent blue

HEWITSON'S BLUE HAIRSTREAK

TAWNY RAJAH

CANOPY
High up in the canopy, butterflies such as Swallowtails, Birdwings, and Morphos abound. The Tawny Rajah flies rapidly in the tree tops where there are fewer predators.

CAMOUFLAGE PATTERNS
To make their leaflike camouflage more realistic, no two African Leaf Butterflies are identical. In the wet season when there are fewer dead leaves around, the Leaf Butterflies rely more on eyespots than camouflage to deter predators.

Distinctive underside looks like a leaf

Central line resembles leaf vein

AFRICAN LEAF BUTTERFLY

GLASSWING BUTTERFLY

Transparent forewing

White hind wing

Glasswing larvae eat passionflower leaves

FOREST FLOOR
Many butterflies and moths shun sunlight, hiding in the darkness of the forest floor. Glasswing butterflies, with their transparent forewings, are almost invisible in the shade. They eat rotting fruit and absorb nutrients from manure or damp ground.

AFRICA

THE SECOND LARGEST AREA of rain forest in the world forms a broad belt across the middle of Africa. The largest butterfly in Africa, *Papilio antimachus*, lives in the tropical rain forests of West Africa; it has a wingspan of up to 10 in (25 cm).

COMMON EMPEROR MOTH

Translucent patch

Eyespot

VERDANT SPHINX MOTH

Streamlined wing

WING MARKINGS
The Common Emperor Moth belongs to a small group of orange, brown, and yellow moths that have a translucent patch on each forewing and prominent eyespots on the hindwings.

GREEN MOTH
This striking Sphinx moth is widespread in African rain forests. The caterpillar, which feeds on the leaves of grapevines and Virginia creepers, has eyespots behind its head to deter predators.

Striking white band

POWERFUL FLIERS
Speedy Palla Butterflies are on the wing all year round in the tropical forests of western, eastern, and central Africa. They have short tails on their hind wings.

PALLA BUTTERFLY

Orange scales on head

AFRICAN MOON MOTH

Metallic rays

Brown markings on long tail

GIANT AFRICAN SKIPPER
This is probably the largest Skipper in the world and has a wingspan of up to 3 ¼ in (8 cm). The striking black-and-white caterpillar feeds on the leaves of cashew trees.

FADED GLORY
The beautiful greens of this spectacular moth fade rapidly in daylight to a yellowish white. This happens to both living and preserved moths. Their eyespots and long tails resemble those of the Moon moths of North America and India.

Black markings of male

Tapered abdomen

MOCKER SWALLOWTAILS
Some forms of the female Mocker Swallowtails mimic foul-tasting Danaid butterflies and have a wide variety of colors. But the males are always pale yellow with black markings and are not mimetic.

ASIA AND AUSTRALASIA

THE HOT, HUMID CLIMATE of southeast Asia, northeast Australia, and Papua New Guinea has encouraged the growth of lush rain forests, where many spectacular butterflies and moths live. Australia and many Asian islands have their own distinct species.

Orange forewing of female

Transparent hindwing

GOLDEN CLEARWING
This wasplike moth from the Northern Territory, Australia, flies quickly in bright sunlight. Males have four transparent wings.

TROPICAL SKIPPER BUTTERFLY
Regent Skippers are unusual both for their bright colors and for the way the males' wings are hooked together like the wings of many moths. They have a swift, jerky flight.

Spray of white scales

Branched antenna of male

HERCULES MOTH

GIANT MOTH
The huge Hercules moth of Northern Australia is related to the Atlas moth. Males have very long tails, while females have broad hind wings with a double lobe instead of a tail.

Long tail – up to 6 ½ in (170 mm)

RAJAH BROOKE'S BIRDWING

SOARING BIRDWING
Rajah Brooke's Birdwing butterflies have a powerful, soaring flight as they speed through the rain forests of Borneo and Malaysia. The boldly colored males often flock to drink from muddy river banks.

Bold triangles of iridescent green

ORANGE SCALES
Waste products react chemically to produce the colors of the Orange Albatross. Males are common on river banks and in forest clearings, but females tend to fly high up in the canopy.

Prominent veins

ORCHID

DOHERTY'S LONGTAIL

ORANGE ALBATROSS

All-orange coloring

Streamerlike hindwing

DEAD OR ALIVE?
If this strange little moth is disturbed, it drops to the ground and pretends to be dead. Doherty's Longtail is a weak flier, active during the day in the rain forests of India and Malaysia.

CENTRAL AND SOUTH AMERICA

THE RAIN FORESTS of Central and South America contain the greatest variety of butterfly and moth species in the world, including the stunning Morphos and Owl butterflies. Many of the butterflies and some of the moths have brilliant iridescent colors.

DIVA MOTH

ZEBRA STRIPES
This Zebra butterfly has warning patterns on its long, narrow fore- and hindwings. This species flies slowly in or near dense forests. If it is disturbed, it makes a creaking sound by wriggling.

Iridescent colors

BLUE THAROPS

DEFENSE TACTICS
The forewings of the large day-flying Diva Moth are camouflaged like a dead leaf. However, the brightly colored hindwings may flash suddenly to startle a predator.

SHINING WINGS
The fast-flying Blue Tharops butterfly belongs to a group of butterflies called Metalmarks, named after the areas of metallic color on their wings.

COLOR MIMIC
Tiger Pierids mimic
the bright warning
colors of the unpleasant-tasting
Danaid butterflies. Their
coloring and behavior vary to
match the different
Danaids they imitate.

TIGER PIERID

Orange
warning color

Complex marblelike
patterns

Wingspan is
9–12 in
(23–30 cm)

GIANT AGRIPPA

FOREST GIANT
The magnificent
Giant Agrippa has the
largest wingspan of any
moth in the world.

QUEEN CRACKER

Blue
metallic
spots

Rounded
hindwing

NOISY FLIGHT
The Queen Cracker butterfly is
named after the clicking noise it
makes when flying. The uppersides
of the wings have iridescent blue
spots. The undersides are
camouflaged, making it hard
to see when settled on a tree.

MORPHOS AND BIRDWINGS

AMONG THE BEST-KNOWN and most spectacular butterflies to flourish in the tropical rain forests are the Morphos of Central and South America and the Birdwings of Asia and Australasia. They are not related, but both have large, iridescent wings and a powerful flight. They fly through the rain-forest canopy or glide along forest paths.

Iridescent upperside

Patterned underside

Rows of eyespots

COMMON MORPHO

Deep brown tips

Blackish brown spots

MOTHER-OF-PEARL MORPHO

PEARLY MORPHO
The delicate, translucent white Mother-of-pearl Morpho occurs only in Brazil. Both males and females have similar colors and patterns. They feed on rotting fruit, especially jackfruit. The caterpillars live in nests in forest trees.

BLUE FLASH
The intense, shimmering blues of male Morphos occur only on the uppersides of the wings. The colors help to attract females and may also serve to dazzle predators when the butterfly needs to escape. Morphos fly in zigzags, beating their wings slowly. Each time the butterfly exposes the darker undersides of its wings, it fades into the background.

GLIDER
The long forewings of this common Birdwing species are ideal for gliding lazily through the treetops. The adults are poisonous and use a warning display to deter predators – while remaining very still, they curve their abdomen downward.

Pointed tip of forewing

Metallic green on male's wings

Yellow body indicates that it is poisonous

CAIRNS BIRDWING

Powerful gliderlike wing

Prominent back vein

Striking wing pattern

Pale abdomen

QUEEN ALEXANDRA'S BIRDWING (FEMALE)

SCARCE
The female Queen Alexandra's Birdwing is the largest known butterfly. Some females have a wingspan of up to 11 in (28 cm). Males are much smaller and more colorful than the females. These butterflies are found only in the rain forests of central and northern Papua New Guinea and are now a rare and protected species.

TROPICAL MOTHS

TWO STRIKING FAMILIES of moths live in the tropical rain forests. The Uraniidae include colorful, day-flying species as well as pale-colored night fliers. The Brahmaeidae are active only at night. They usually have large eyespots to frighten off predators and a well-developed proboscis for feeding.

Threadlike antenna of female

MADAGASCAN SUNSET MOTH

Rainbowlike colors

SUNSET COLORS
The shape and brilliant colors of this day-flying moth give it a striking resemblance to a Swallowtail butterfly. The caterpillar's habit of eating poisonous plants and the bright colors of the adult indicate that the Madagascan Sunset Moth may contain poisons. Victorians used its multicolored wings to make jewelry.

STRIPED PROTECTION
The striped wings of this small, night-flying Uraniid help to break up its outline, camouflaging the moth while it rests during the day. Its slender body is similar to those of its relatives, the Geometer moths. The *Cyphura pardata* lives only in Papua New Guinea and the neighboring islands.

Striped forewing

Distracting eyespots

CYPHURA PARDATA

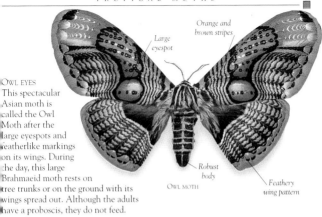

Large
eyespot

Orange and
brown stripes

OWL EYES
This spectacular
Asian moth is
called the Owl
Moth after the
large eyespots and
featherlike markings
on its wings. During
the day, this large
Brahmaeid moth rests on
tree trunks or on the ground with its
wings spread out. Although the adults
have a proboscis, they do not feed.

Robust
body

OWL MOTH

Feathery
wing pattern

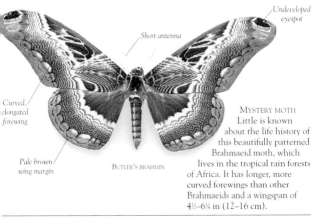

Undeveloped
eyespot

Short antenna

Curved,
elongated
forewing

Pale brown
wing margin

BUTLER'S BRAHMIN

MYSTERY MOTH
Little is known
about the life history of
this beautifully patterned
Brahmaeid moth, which
lives in the tropical rain forests
of Africa. It has longer, more
curved forewings than other
Brahmaeids and a wingspan of
4½–6¼ in (12–16 cm).

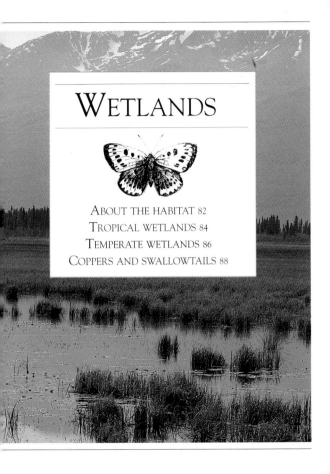

WETLANDS

ABOUT THE HABITAT

WHILE FEW BUTTERFLIES and moths live on open water, some species are attracted to the plants that grow in wetland habitats. These frequently occur near rivers, lakes, and seas. Temporary wetlands, caused by seasonal flooding, also attract some species.

WETLAND HABITATS
Six percent of the Earth's surface is covered by wetlands. These habitats occur in tropical and temperate regions and include mangrove swamps, peat bogs, and marshes.

LEAF SHELTER
The eggs of the Brown China-mark Moth are laid on water plantain. When they hatch, the caterpillars mine into the leaves. Later, they use pieces of leaf to make small shelters in which they live.

BROWN CHINA-MARK MOTH

Delicate patterning

VICEROY

Black cross-line on hind wing

Slender abdomen

VICEROY
These American butterflies can often be seen by riversides, canals, lakeshores, and over marshes, flapping their wings wildly in between brief glides. They lay their eggs on trees such as willow and aspen. The Viceroy is also known as the Mimic butterfly because it closely resembles the Monarch.

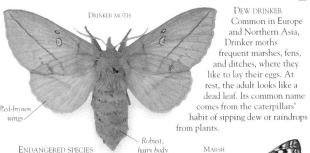

DRINKER MOTH

DEW DRINKER
Common in Europe and Northern Asia, Drinker moths frequent marshes, fens, and ditches, where they like to lay their eggs. At rest, the adult looks like a dead leaf. Its common name comes from the caterpillars' habit of sipping dew or raindrops from plants.

Red-brown wings

Robust, hairy body

ENDANGERED SPECIES
Due to the drainage of wet meadows for agriculture, Marsh Fritillaries are rapidly declining throughout Europe and temperate Asia. They live in isolated colonies in damp meadows and on marshy hillsides, where the caterpillars' food plant, devil's-bit scabious, grows.

MARSH FRITILLARY

Intricate patterning on wings

COMMON EGGFLY

Weak fliers that do not stray far

TROPICAL SWAMPS
The Common Eggfly butterfly is attracted to a wide variety of habitats from India to New Zealand, including the mangrove swamps that occur along the tropical coasts of Malaysia and Australia.

Toothlike markings on wing margin

WETLAND FACTS

• The wetlands are home to a rich diversity of plant life.

• Wetlands are at risk from pollution and drainage and are disappearing rapidly all over the world.

• Tropical mangrove trees have aerial breathing roots that stick out of the water.

TROPICAL WETLANDS

THESE HOT, HUMID regions are rich in plant and animal life. However, competition for food is severe. Some butterflies and moths are able to live in tropical swamps. The caterpillars feed on mangrove trees that thrive in waterlogged soil and on aquatic plants, such as papyrus.

Shiny white background

WHITE PEACOCK

VARIOUS FORMS
This butterfly flourishes in the swamps of tropical North America, and in South and Central America. Many forms occur, differing in color and pattern. The spiny, silver-spotted caterpillar eats water hyssop.

An unusually dull-colored Tiger moth

WATER TIGER MOTH

UNDERWATER
The caterpillar of the South American Water Tiger moth not only lives underwater, but can swim. It traps air in dense hairs that cover its body.

PIRATE BUTTERFLY

Purple wash on males

SEASONAL CHANGE
The Pirate Butterfly lives in the African swamps and shows seasonal changes in color. The dry season brood has dark brown wing undersides, while the wet season brood has pale brown undersides.

Row of blue-black spots

LARGE TREE
NYMPH BUTTERFLY

WEAK FLIER
The strikingly
patterned Large Tree
Nymph butterfly is
widespread in southern
Asia and Japan. Although
a species of the forests, it
lives in mangrove swamps in
the southern part of its
range. In dappled sunlight,
this slow-flying butterfly is
almost invisible.

*Zigzag
markings*

*Slender
body*

*Veins outlined
in brown*

*Violet-blue wings
of male*

WIDELY DISTRIBUTED
Tiny African Grass Blues range from
southwestern Europe through Africa
and Asia to Australia. They live in
wetland and grassland habitats in both
tropical and temperate areas. The
caterpillars are green and covered with
short hairs. They feed on devil's thorn.

*Thin,
brown
margin*

AFRICAN GRASS BLUE

White spots

*Orange warning colors
(not common to all the
forms of this species)*

BLACK-AND-WHITE TIGER
This species lives in the mangrove
swamps of Malaysia. There are
many forms that live in different
geographical regions from
Southeast Asia to Australia. The
caterpillars of the Australian form
feed on poisonous milkweeds in
brackish (slightly salty) water.

BLACK-AND-WHITE
TIGER BUTTERFLY

TEMPERATE WETLANDS

MOTHS AND BUTTERFLIES are attracted to a variety of plants that grow in flat, marshy meadows. Many species flourish among reeds and bulrushes and on willow and alder trees. Only a few species can live in peat bogs, such as those in Alaska, Ireland, and New Zealand, where the plant life is limited to damp mosses.

Distinctive black markings

Dark brown borders

INSECT EATER
The Harvester butterfly is closely associated with alder swamps in Canada and the US. The adult butterfly drinks the honeydew produced by aphids, while the caterpillar feeds on Woolly aphids found on alder trees.

HARVESTER BUTTERFLY

Clubbed antenna

Solid black margins

TYPICAL FRITILLARY
In much of Europe and temperate Asia, the Lesser Marbled Fritillary can be found in marshy areas where meadowsweet and great burnet grow. These are the food plants of its caterpillars. The wings of the adults have typical Fritillary markings – black spots on an orange background.

Scalloped edge LESSER MARBLED FRITILLARY

Metallic specks

SWAMP METALMARK

Black lines and spots

ALDER

White patch on forewing

LARGE CHECKERED SKIPPER

THISTLE DIET
The Swamp Metalmark, as its name implies, occurs in wet meadows and swamps in Pennsylvania, the Great Lakes, and Minnesota. The female lays eggs on the caterpillar's food plant, bog thistle.

LARGE CHECKERED SKIPPER
This fast-flying butterfly is found in marshy meadows from southern Scandinavia to the Mediterranean. It often lives in small isolated colonies. The caterpillars feed on various grasses.

Purplish-pink band on forewing

Pale yellow hind wing

PINK-BARRED SALLOW MOTH

SALLOW MOTH
Despite its name, the brightly colored Pink-barred Sallow moth is yellow with red or purple bands on the forewings. It is widely distributed in Europe and Asia and is also found in Canada and the US. The eggs are laid on willow trees and the caterpillar feeds on willow catkins and other damp-meadow plants.

COPPERS AND SWALLOWTAILS

SOME SPECIES OF Coppers and Swallowtails live and breed in wetland habitats. Coppers are small, swift fliers – their iridescent wings flash in the sun. The large Swallowtail butterflies tend to have a slow, flapping flight, but they can also be brightly colored.

Duller colors of female

LARGE COPPER FEMALE

Brighter colors of male LARGE COPPER MALE

MAGNIFICENT MALES

In common with other members of the Lycaenidae, male and female Coppers are often different colors. The males of the Large Copper, which lives in wet meadows and marshes, are a much brighter orange-red than the duller females. The caterpillars feed on dock plants, especially water dock.

Purple patches

PURPLE-EDGED COPPER

HABITAT THREAT

Both the Purple-edged Copper and the Large Copper have declined in number, a their marshy habitats have been drained for cultivation. They hibernate as young caterpillars and resume feeding in spring.

Bold pattern

Black band dusted with blue

Red eyespots

SWALLOWTAIL

SWALLOWTAIL
This species of Swallowtail, known in the US as the Old World Swallowtail, is one of the few Swallowtails to occur outside the tropics. In Britain, Swallowtails live in the reed beds of the Norfolk Broads; their pupae may be found attached to reed stems.

Distinctive white stripes

ZEBRA SWALLOWTAIL

KITE BUTTERFLY
The Zebra Swallowtail is the most common of the Kite Swallowtails, named after their triangular wings and long tails. Zebra Swallowtails live in moist, shaded, lowland woods. There are several generations a year; the adults that emerge in spring have shorter tails and are smaller and whiter than the later broods.

Long tails on hind wings

GRASSLANDS
AND BARRENS

ABOUT THE HABITAT

GRASSY HABITATS ARE important breeding grounds. There are plenty of grasses on which the caterpillars can feed and many flowers to attract butterflies and moths. On windy days, they find it hard to fly in open grasslands and shelter low down among the grasses.

MEADOW BROWN

Scalloped edge

IN THE LONG GRASS
Brown butterflies, such as this Meadow Brown, prefer medium to tall grass. Their caterpillars hide deep in grass clumps by day and climb up the stems to eat the juicy tips after dark.

SILVER-STUDDED BLUE

Spotted underside

HEATHLAND BUTTERFLIES
Blues, such as the Silver-Studded Blue, frequent low-growing grasslands and heathlands. Most heaths have poor soils and are dominated by heather plants; grasses grow in the wetter areas.

Furry, brown thorax

Black markings

Red hind wings

GARDEN VISITOR
Although brightly colored, the Garden Tiger Moth flies mainly at night. As its common name suggests, it frequents gardens, where the female lays her eggs on a wide variety of plants.

GARDEN TIGER MOTH

Striking eyespot

Iridescent violet iris

Orange bands

BUCKEYE BUTTERFLY

SHORELINE VISITORS
In autumn, hordes of Buckeyes migrate southward along the east coast of the United States. They live and breed in open fields and scrubland. The adults hibernate during the winter.

GRASSLAND FACTS

• Farming and building projects threaten areas of grassland and barrens.

• Agricultural fields do not contain the right species of plants for many species to survive.

• Grassland species include Browns, Blues, Skippers, Burnets, and Grass moths.

GUINEA FOWL BUTTERFLY

AFRICAN SCRUBLAND
A common sight in the African bush is the Guineafowl Butterfly, so called because its spotted wings resemble Guineafowl feathers. It flies close to the ground and rests with its wings outspread.

Black and white spots

Silvery white wings of male

GHOST MOTH

GHOSTLY PEST
The male Ghost Moth's shiny white wings attract females as he flies over meadows at dusk. The caterpillars feed on the roots of grasses and other plants and can become agricultural pests.

Butterflies are attracted to broad flowers, like this dandelion

COASTAL REGIONS

SAND DUNES, GRASSLANDS, and barrens near the coast
provide favorable habitats for butterflies and moths,
especially in sheltered locations where wild herbs and
flowers grow. Building, tourism, and intensive farming
along coasts has reduced
the diversity of species.

TWO-TAILED
PASHA

*Pale inner
margins*

Tails

MAQUIS BUTTERFLY
The fast-flying Two-tailed
Pasha is the only European
butterfly with two tails. It lives in
Mediterranean barrens (*maquis*), but
also occurs in southern Africa.

CLEOPATRA
This beautiful yellow southern
European species is found in
scrubby coastal regions of North
Africa. Although the adults mate
before hibernating, the females do
not lay their eggs until the spring.

*Conspicuous
red markings*

SPANISH
FESTOON

*Zigzag
pattern*

TAILLESS SWALLOWTAIL
The Spanish Festoon is a
Swallowtail without the long tails
typical of its relatives. It flies from
February to May among the rough,
dry barrens of the hilly Mediterranean
coast of southwest Europe.

CLEOPATRA BUTTERFLY

Pointed tip

*Orange
patch on
forewing of
male*

PAINTED SKIPPER

Orange patch

Striped abdomen

POISONOUS BODY

White Ermine moths inhabit coastal dunes in Europe, Asia, and Japan. Their colorful, poisonous abdomens stand out against their white wings. The hairy caterpillars can move at high speed.

STRIPED CATERPILLARS

Mainly found on the Australian coasts of Queensland and Victoria, the Painted Skipper can also be seen in the Blue Mountains in New South Wales. The caterpillars have striped bodies to camouflage them among the sword grasses on which they live.

WHITE ERMINE

Warning colors on abdomen

DUNE GEM

Common Opal butterflies live among the sand dunes of southern Africa. The male can be distinguished from the female by the extensive blue patches on his copper wings.

COMMON OPAL

Copper margins

Opalescent blue

Pointed tip to hind wing

SEAMAY

SAVANNA AND BUSH

THE BUTTERFLIES AND MOTHS
of the African savanna,
Australian bush, and Asian
scrub have to survive dry
seasons, or follow the rain to
where plants are plentiful.
Larvae and pupae often
remain dormant during
the hot summer.

EUCALYPTUS

*White
club o
antenn*

White spots

PALM
SKIPPER

DATE AT DUSK
When dusk comes to the Afric
savanna, Palm Skippers with
their distinctive white wing
spots, fly near phoenix date
palms, on which their
caterpillars feed.

*Also called
Blue Argus*

BLUE PANSY
This butterfly can be seen
flitting about in hot
sunshine in a variety of
habitats, including bush
areas in Africa, Australia,
and Asia.

BANKSIA
MOTH

Black markin

*Eyespots
on blue
hind wing*

BLUE PANSY
(MALE)

DEFENSE
The spotted
caterpillar of the
Australian Banksia Moth
feeds during the day on the
leaves of banksia and hakea
plants. If disturbed, the front
part of its body rears up.

*Yellow-
orange tufts*

96

DARK CHOPPER MOTH

Sharply angled hind wing

Abdomen has pale, hairlike scales

IRRITATING HAIR
Caterpillars of the Dark Chopper feed on acacia and other plants of the African savanna. Their bodies are covered with hairs that can irritate human skin. This moth gets its name from the male's sharply angled hind wings.

LARGE BLUE CHARAXES

Spots on forewing

STRONG WINGS
Powerful fliers from the tropical African scrub, Large Blue Charaxes feed on rotten fruit or tree sap. The males also visit patches of mud to absorb nutrients. The caterpillars are green and feed on mahogany beans.

Small pointed tails

YELLOW COSTER

Forewings darker than hind wings

Wings slightly iridescent

ACACIA

BAD TASTE
Predators find the caterpillars of the Yellow Coster from southern Asia doubly disgusting. They feed on poisonous plants, giving them a bad taste, and they also give off a foul smell. They assemble in groups to maximize the stink.

TEMPERATE GRASSLANDS

WITH THEIR MANY kinds of wildflowers and grasses, temperate grasslands are ideal habitats. Warm, south-facing chalk and limestone slopes are home to a particularly rich variety of moths and butterflies.

MARBLED WHITE

Checkered black-and-white pattern

Eyespot

Scalloped hind wing

WALL BROWN

CHECKERED WINGS
A member of the Browns, the Marbled White butterfly feeds on flowers such as thistles. Early and late in the day, it may be seen resting on grassheads, holding its checkered wings open.

SUNBATHER
The Wall or Wall Brown is named after its habit of basking on sunny walls, short grass, and bare soil. With its wings closed, it blends well with the bare ground.

ORANGE TIP

Only the male has eye-catching orange tips

SPRING BUTTERFLIES
Orange Tips are found in Europe and Asia. Both sexes show the mottled green undersides of their wings as they drink from spring flowers.

ADONIS BLUE

BEAUTIFUL BLUE
Widespread throughout Europe, the
Adonis Blue is named after the
handsome boy loved by the Greek
goddess, Aphrodite. It lives in colonies
on chalk and limestone grasslands and
feeds on wildflowers. Males often gather
to feed on animal droppings.

SMALL COPPER

Black forewing markings

Black-and-white wing fringes

INTRUDERS BEWARE!
One of the most common species
in the northern hemisphere, the
Small Copper is often found near
flowers, basking in the sun with its
wings open. Males are apt to chase
away other butterflies that intrude
into their territory. The camouflaged
caterpillars feed on dock leaves.

CHALK GRASSLANDS
The Silver-spotted Skipper can be
seen on grazed, chalk grasslands
in Europe. The caterpillar
lives in a rolled-up leaf
blade and forms a cocoon
from grass and soil.

SILVER-SPOTTED SKIPPER

Curved tip to antenna

FIELDS, PARKS, AND GARDENS

A WIDE RANGE of butterflies and moths visits these man-made habitats, which often contain plants that also grow in natural grasslands. They provide useful feeding stations for passing moths and butterflies.

Dark eyespots

CECROPIA

Red and white bands on body

GARDEN GIANT
Found from March to June in fields and gardens in the US and southern Canada, the *Cecropia* (also called the Robin Moth because of its red body) is the largest North American moth.

Yellow spotting

CITRUS SWALLOWTAIL

UNWELCOME GUEST
Christmas in South Africa often brings the Citrus Swallowtail, also called the Christmas butterfly. However, its arrival is not welcomed by gardeners since its caterpillars are highly destructive pests of citrus trees, peas, and beans.

CATERPILLAR DISGUISE
Brimstone Moths can be seen at dusk in northern European gardens and around hedgerows. They lay their eggs on hawthorn and blackthorn. The caterpillars are very well camouflaged – when they keep still, they look like twigs.

Hair-like scales

BRIMSTONE MOTH

CABBAGE WHITES

Large Whites, also known as Cabbage Whites, are common in vegetable gardens and cabbage fields in Europe. They lay their eggs on cabbage or nasturtium plants. The pupae overwinter in sheltered spots and the adults emerge in April.

Black wing tips

LARGE WHITE

ROBUST HAWKMOTH

Across Europe and Asia, the Elephant Hawkmoth may be seen speeding from flower to flower at dusk. Its long tongue probes into deep-throated flowers. The large caterpillars feed on fuchsia in gardens and parks.

Sturdy legs have spurs

Pink and olive-brown stripes

ELEPHANT HAWKMOTH

GARDEN BUTTERFLY

The Small Tortoiseshell is common in European gardens, and can be seen resting on flowers or near patches of nettles, on which it lays its eggs. The undersides of its wings are camouflaged to look like tree bark.

SMALL TORTOISESHELL

Points on edges of forewing and hind wing

Hebe plants attract a wide variety of butterflies

SKIPPERS

SUNNY, TROPICAL, AND TEMPERATE grasslands are home
to about 3,000 species of mothlike butterflies known a
Skippers. Their common name comes from the way
they busily skip from flower to flower. Most are small,
with dull brown or orange-brown coloring. Their
caterpillars usually feed on grass, living and pupating
inside rolled-up leaves, drawn together with silk.

SKIPPER SHAPE
A typical Skipper has a large
head, thick body, and short,
triangular-shaped forewings.
The antennae, which are
widely separated at the base,
usually have swollen or curved
tips that end with a point.
Skipper caterpillars have
a large head, a thin neck, and
a body that tapers at each end.

Angular forewing

Curved tip

GRIZZLED SKIPPER

Large, rounded hind wing

Delicate patterning

DINGY SKIPPER

LAZY SUNBATHERS
Dingy Skippers live in small colonies
on grassy hills and open heaths in
Europe and Asia. They spend long
periods basking in the sunshine, with their
wings held open. At night, or in cold
weather, they rest on the tops of grasses,
draping their wings around the stems.

SILK SPINNERS
Large Skippers spend much of their time
establishing territorial bases. The
caterpillars shelter, hibernate, and
pupate inside a tube made of grass
blades, wrapped with cords of silk.

Visible
veins

LARGE SKIPPER

Small head
Prominent
eye

YUCCA SKIPPERS
These large skippers with stout
abdomens are found only in
southern parts of the US and
Central America. They differ
from other skippers in that they
have smaller heads and antennae
that are set relatively close at the
base.

Stout body

YUCCA GIANT SKIPPER

Point at tip

White patches
on forewing

LONG-TAILS
The hind wings of some
Skippers in the Americas are
elongated into long tails, not
unlike those of the Swallowtail
butterflies. The Long-tailed
Skipper can be distinguished from
other Long-tails in North America
by the iridescent green-blue on the
upperside of the wings. The larva
feeds on wild and cultivated beans
and is known as the "Bean Leaf
Roller" or the "Roller Worm."

Hairlike
scales

Elongated
hind wing

LONG-TAILED SKIPPER

DAY-FLYING MOTHS

OFTEN MISTAKEN FOR BUTTERFLIES, colorful day-flying moths abound in summer meadows and pastures. Many have conspicuous warning colors to tell predators that they are poisonous or that they taste unpleasant. As they fly from flower to flower seeking nectar to drink, some day fliers bear a striking resemblance to birds, bees, and wasps.

POISONOUS PLANTS
Striking Cinnabar Moths obtain their poisons from the caterpillar's food plant. Large numbers of this species' orange and black caterpillars are often seen feeding on poisonous ragwort plants. When ready to pupate, they burrow underground.

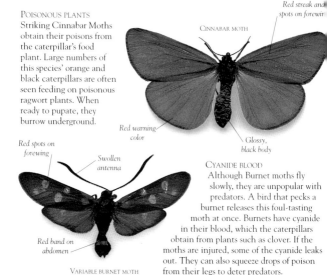

Red streak and spots on forewing

CINNABAR MOTH

Red warning color

Glossy, black body

Red spots on forewing

Swollen antenna

Red band on abdomen

VARIABLE BURNET MOTH

CYANIDE BLOOD
Although Burnet moths fly slowly, they are unpopular with predators. A bird that pecks a burnet releases this foul-tasting moth at once. Burnets have cyanide in their blood, which the caterpillars obtain from plants such as clover. If the moths are injured, some of the cyanide leaks out. They can also squeeze drops of poison from their legs to deter predators.

TIGER MOTHS
Some colorful Tiger
moths synthesize their
own poisons. Their
caterpillars feed on a
variety of harmless plants,
and are protected by
unappetizing hairs rather
than by poisons. The
larvae are commonly
known as "Woolly Bears."

*Greenish black
forewing*

SCARLET TIGER

*Black central
stripe*

BIRD OR MOTH?
The hum of its rapidly beating
wings and its darting flight give
the Hummingbird Hawkmoth its
remarkable resemblance to
a hummingbird. These tiny moths
hover in front of flowers, sucking up
nectar with a long proboscis.

*"Tail-fan" is like that
of a hummingbird*

*Robust
body*

HUMMINGBIRD
HAWKMOTH

Scaleless wing

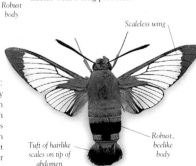

BEE MIMIC
With its clear wings and furry
body, the King's Bee Hawkmoth resembles
a bee. When the moth
emerges from its pupa, its wings
are completely covered with
scales, but these fall off when it
flies. Quickly darting from flower
to flower, these moths also
behave like bees.

*Tuft of hairlike
scales on tip of
abdomen*

*Robust,
beelike
body*

KING'S BEE HAWKMOTH

WHITES AND SULPHURS

BLACK-VEINED WHITE

THESE BUTTERFLIES are found in open, sunny places where their caterpillars' food plants are available. The markings and colors of Whites and Sulphurs vary during the year, being darker in summer.

DECLINING NUMBERS

The Black-Veined White used to be common across Europe and temperate Asia in orchards and hedgerows. It has mysteriously declined in number. The caterpillars hibernate in a communal silk nest.

SMALL BUT WIDE-RANGING

Often seen fluttering in gardens across the Northern hemisphere and also in Australia, the Cabbage Butterfly is one of the most widely distributed butterflies. Its caterpillars damage cabbages and some garden flowers.

Grey shading

CABBAGE BUTTERFLY

BATH WHITE

SUMMER VISITOR

A regular summer migrant from southern Europe and North Africa to many parts of northern Europe, the Bath White prefers warm, dry grasslands. Although a rare visitor to Britain, it is named after the city in southwestern England. The undersides of its wings have olive-green markings.

ORANGE SPOTS
Caterpillars of the Orange Sulphur are pests of the alfalfa crop and also feed on clovers. The species is common in many parts of the US and Mexico. The color of the adults varies, but they always have an orange spot on their hind wings, which distinguishes them from the Common Sulphur.

ORANGE SULPHUR

Orange spot

CLOUDLESS SULPHUR

Black spotting at wing edge

ONE-WAY TRAVELER
In summer, the Cloudless Sulphur migrates northward from Mexico and the southern US. Large and fast-flying, it covers great distances, traveling around the Caribbean or up to New York. The migrants do not live long enough to return south. The reason for this mass migration is unknown.

Brown markings

Fast, powerful fliers

Orange wing tip

SECRETIVE FEMALES
There are usually two generations a year of Great Orange Tip butterflies; the wet season brood tends to be larger than the dry season generation. While the males prefer open country, the females live mainly in the forests. When they rest on the ground, they mimic dead leaves.

GREAT ORANGE TIP

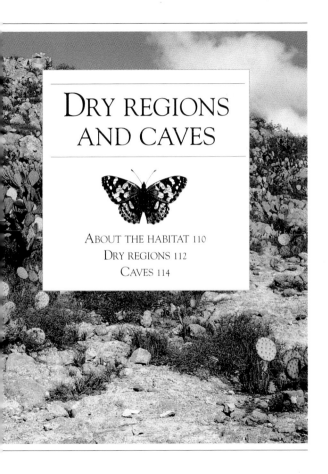

DRY REGIONS
AND CAVES

ABOUT THE HABITAT

DRY REGIONS ARE characterized by low rainfall, extreme temperatures, and sparse vegetation. Only hardy moths and butterflies can survive such hostile environments. Many species seek refuge in damp, dark caves, where the temperature remains constant throughout the year.

Pointed tip on hind wing

LITTLE
TIGER BLUE

TIGER BLUE
The Little Tiger
Blue butterfly lives
in hot, dry regions
the Near and Middle East.
The caterpillars feed on the
jujube bush – a small, tough, spiny
shrub, also known as Christ's thorn.

Ringlet around eyespot

Robust proboscis to pierce tough plants

AFRICAN RINGLET
Widespread throughout Africa, south of the
Sahara, and southwest Asia, the African
Ringlet has an eye-catching, bouncing flight.
Its short, sturdy proboscis helps it to suck
water from the tough stems of desert plants.

Nutritious animal droppings

PEACOCK
For many moths and butterflies, caves provide shelter from harsh weather conditions. The Peacock butterfly hibernates as an adult in caves during the cold, northern winter. The dark undersides of its wings help to camouflage it from predators such as birds and bats.

PEACOCK
BUTTERFLY

Camouflaged
undersides

WITCHETTY GRUBS
Several species of Australian ghost moth larvae feed on the roots of plants in arid regions. The large caterpillars, known as Witchetty grubs, are eaten by some Aboriginal peoples.

This is one of the Ghost
moths that produce
Witchetty grubs

Green foreleg

Crimson pigments
produced by body's
waste products

SPLENDID GHOST
MOTH

VARIATIONS
The Crimson Tip butterfly is found in arid, thornbush land in Africa, the Near East, and India. Its appearance varies according to the season and region.

CRIMSON TIP

DESERT FACTS
• To prevent water loss, plants in semideserts have small leaves.

• Oases in deserts are a vital lifeline for animal life.

• Overgrazing can turn dry grasslands into deserts.

DRY REGIONS

VAST AREAS OF SEMIDESERT occur on most continents. The hot, dry days can lead to rapid water loss and death for many butterflies and moths. Many species migrate in search of rain. Others survive by feeding on tough, thorny desert plants that store water in their stems to protect against drought.

Feeding on yucca leaves

YUCCA SKIPPERS
Yucca Skipper butterflies of Central and South America do not feed as adults, although related species sometimes drink from moist ground. Their caterpillars bore into the fleshy stems, leaves, or roots of yuccas and agaves.

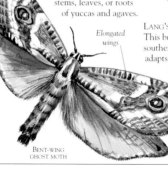

Elongated wings

LANG'S SHORT-TAILED BLUE
This butterfly lives in a variety of habitats southern Europe and the Middle East. It adapts to dry climates and is often seen fluttering in dry Mediterranean scr

Tiny

DESERT GHOST
The large Australian Bent-wing Ghost moth sometimes leaves its forest habitat, and can be spotted shimmering across the desert at dusk.

BENT-WING
GHOST MOTH

Threadlike antenna of female

Red and black speckles

Brown markings

CRIMSON SPECKLED MOTH

MIGRATION

Crimson Speckled Moths occur in Africa, southern Europe, and the Middle East. In desert areas, they gravitate toward oases. This is a migratory species and occasionally Crimson Speckled Moths have reached Britain. However, they cannot survive the cold, northern winter.

CACTUS

Black margins on pink forewings

WHITE-LINED SPHINX

WIDE RANGE

The powerful, fast-flying White-lined Sphinx can survive in dry areas, but like many other migratory species, it occurs in a wide variety of habitats throughout North and South America, Europe, Africa, Asia, and Australia. It is both a day- and night-flying species.

Water stored in stem

CAVES

THE TEMPERATURE IN caves remains almost constant throughout the year. In harsh environments, caves are ideal places for moths and butterflies to hibernate or estivate (lie dormant during hot, dry summer months). Some small moths spend their entire lives in caves, feeding on the droppings of bats and other animals.

Colors blend with rocks

ALPINE CAVES
In spring, Bogong Moths gather in caves and rock crevices in the Australian Alps. They remain dormant during the hot, dry summer. Their gray-brown coloring helps to conceal them from predators.

Camouflaged like a dead leaf to protect them from being eaten

CAMOUFLAGE
Comma butterflies are characterized by ragged wing margins that help to camouflage them. They hibernate during the winter, sometimes resting on sheltered tree trunks or hiding in caves throughout Europe, North Africa, and temperate Asia. The butterflies emerge in the spring to mate and lay their eggs.

COMMA BUTTERFLY

HERALD MOTH
This widespread moth ranges from
Canada and the US, across Europe
to Japan. The caterpillar feeds on
willow, and the adult uses small barbs
on its proboscis to pierce fruit. During
the northern winter, the adults
hibernate in caves.

COMMON BROWN
BUTTERFLY

Long, hairlike
scales maintain
body heat
during
hibernation

Scalloped
hind wing

Eyespot

Herald moth rests
against rock of cave

SURVIVING THE HEAT
After mating, the male of this Australian butterfly
dies in the summer heat. However, the female
Common Brown flies off to find
shelter, sometimes in the entrances
of caves. She estivates over the
summer and reemerges later in the
year to produce another generation.

Drab-colored
wings

DAYTIME RETREAT
The night-flying Old Lady Moth is
known in Europe for its habit of
creeping behind shutters and
curtains or hiding in sheds or caves
during daylight hours.

OLD LADY MOTH

ARCTIC AND MOUNTAINS

ABOUT THE HABITAT

IN THE SEVERE CLIMATES of Arctic and mountain habitats, there are fierce winds, intensely cold winters, and very short summers. Moths and butterflies have adapted for survival against the elements as well as for protection against predators. Many fly only when the air is still, making short, low flights from one shelter to another.

ANTIFREEZE
Many Arctic species, such as this Arctic Clouded Yellow butterfly, have a type of "antifreeze" in their blood to help them survive freezing temperatures.

MOUNTAIN AND ARCTIC

• Some butterflies live at altitudes of over 16,400 ft (5,000 m).

• Caterpillars of some Arctic and mountain species can take over three years to mature.

• Some pupae may be frozen and thawed several times.

ANTLER MOTH
Named after the antlerlike markings on the forewings, the Antler Moth flies by day and at night. It occurs in Asia, Siberia, and North America on upland moors at altitudes up to 6,560 ft (2,000 m).

Yellow streaks on forewings

ANTLER MOTH

Pa.. fring..

White band

THE HERMIT

White spots

PIEDMONT RINGLET

THE HERMIT BUTTERFLY
The mottled coloring of the Hermit helps to camouflage it on the bare, rocky mountainsides of Europe. The caterpillar feeds mainly on blue moor grass and hibernates during the winter.

RINGLET

Black rings

The dark colors of the Piedmont Ringlet help this butterfly absorb as much sunshine as possible. In June and July, it flies over the stony, grassy slopes of mountains in southern Europe at 5,000–6,000 ft (1,520–1,830 m) above sea level.

Orange patch

COMMON WALL BUTTERFLY

Black-and-white spots

LOW FLIER
The Common Wall butterfly of Iran, India, and western China lives on sunny mountainsides above 6,560 ft (2,000 m). To avoid being blown by winds, it flies close to the ground.

NOW YOU SEE IT
The Silver butterfly inhabits high mountain areas of the Andes. Its silvery wings are reflective, making the butterfly shine brightly and then seemingly disappear in the light.

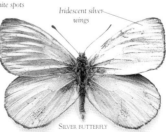

Iridescent silver wings

SILVER BUTTERFLY

ARCTIC AND TUNDRA

DURING THE BRIEF Arctic summer, the snow melts and flowers bloom on the windswept, treeless tundra. A few hardy species of butterflies and moths emerge to take advantage of the long days and feed on the flowers. Many Arctic species are small and hairy.

CATERPILLAR OF GARDEN TIGER MOTH

Called "Woolly Bear" after its hairy appearance

ARCTIC FRITILLARY

Dark markings absorb sunlight

Brown spots and bars

WOOLLY COAT
This caterpillar sometime basks in the sun. The dark colors of the "Woolly Bear" caterpillar help to absorb the weak northern sunshine. Its long, hairy coat traps body warmth.

ICE EDGE
The Arctic Fritillary lives in tundra from the US across northern Europe to Asia, and has been found farther north than any other species of fritillary. is one of only about six species of butterfly to survive in Greenland, where it lives on strips of greenery that skirt a thick layer of ice.

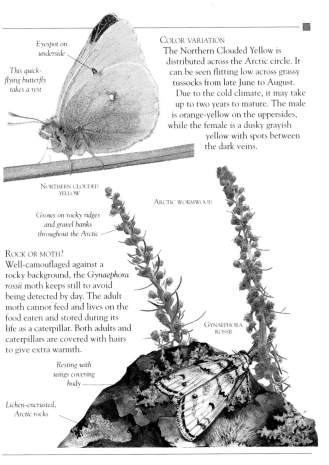

Eyespot on underside

This quick-flying butterfly takes a rest

COLOR VARIATION

The Northern Clouded Yellow is distributed across the Arctic circle. It can be seen flitting low across grassy tussocks from late June to August. Due to the cold climate, it may take up to two years to mature. The male is orange-yellow on the uppersides, while the female is a dusky grayish yellow with spots between the dark veins.

NORTHERN CLOUDED YELLOW

ARCTIC WORMWOOD

Grows on rocky ridges and gravel banks throughout the Arctic

ROCK OR MOTH?

Well-camouflaged against a rocky background, the *Gynaephora rossii* moth keeps still to avoid being detected by day. The adult moth cannot feed and lives on the food eaten and stored during its life as a caterpillar. Both adults and caterpillars are covered with hairs to give extra warmth.

GYNAEPHORA ROSSII

Resting with wings covering body

Lichen-encrusted, Arctic rocks

MOUNTAIN MOORLANDS

MOORLANDS cover mountainsides with a blanket of low-growing plants, including moss, heather, coarse grass, and bilberry. Weather conditions out on the moors are often very cold, wet, and windy, but several species of moths and butterflies have adapted to this harsh environment and can survive the long winters.

MOORLAND CLOUDED YELLOW

THREATENED SPECIES
Once widespread on upland moors in Europe and North America, the Moorland Clouded Yellow has declined in number. Its habitats are threatened by the spread of agricultural land and conifer plantations.

Brown margin

DRYAD BUTTERFLY

Blue center to eyespot

MOORLAND BOUNCER
The dark brown Dryad butterfly bounces as it flies over moorland meadows in Europe and temperate Asia. The female lays her eggs on grasses, such as purple moor grass. The caterpillars feed at night and hibernate in the winter.

LARGE HEATH BUTTERFLY

LARGE HEATH

On dull, wet days, Large Heaths rest low down on moorland grasses, with their wings folded tightly over their backs. They live in large colonies; the males are more conspicuous than the females, which tend to hide behind tussocks of grass.

Large Heaths vary in color in different areas

Row of eyespots

LEAF MINER

The iridescent, green Forester moth lives in boggy moorland in Europe, right up to the Arctic circle. Like its relative the Burnet moth, it flies by day. The young caterpillars feed on sorrel, mining between the upper and lower surfaces of the leaves.

Feathered antenna of male

HEATHER

THE FORESTER

Blackish hind wings are typical of all Foresters

Underside washed with green

DARK GREEN FRITILLARY

FAST FLIERS

Moorland forms of the Dark Green Fritillary have evolved large, dusky wings to help them absorb the sun's rays. They are fast and powerful fliers and live at heights of over 9,840 ft (3,000 m).

MOUNTAIN FORESTS

THE VEGETATION growing on mountainsides changes with the altitude. Warmer, deciduous forests on the lower slopes give way to cooler, coniferous forests higher up. These different forest habitats are home to a fascinating variety of butterflies and moths, including some of the most spectacular *Lepidoptera* in the world.

SPRUCE CONES
Typical of mountain forests are evergreen coniferous trees, such as pines, spruces, and firs.

Branched antenna

Veins marked with red-brown scales

Multicolored eyespot

MOON MOTH
The beautiful Spanish Moon Moth is an inhabitant of pine forests in the mountains of central Spain and the Pyrenees. It flies during the day and also at night at altitudes of up to 5,900 ft (1,800 m). The caterpillar eats the needles of various species of pine.

Males have long, curved hind tail

Long, brown hairy scales for warmth

SPANISH MOON MOTH

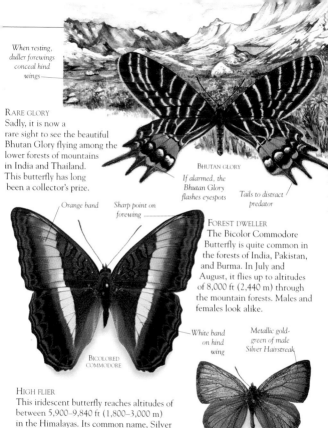

When resting, duller forewings conceal hind wings

RARE GLORY
Sadly, it is now a rare sight to see the beautiful Bhutan Glory flying among the lower forests of mountains in India and Thailand. This butterfly has long been a collector's prize.

BHUTAN GLORY

If alarmed, the Bhutan Glory flashes eyespots

Tails to distract predator

Orange band

Sharp point on forewing

FOREST DWELLER
The Bicolor Commodore Butterfly is quite common in the forests of India, Pakistan, and Burma. In July and August, it flies up to altitudes of 8,000 ft (2,440 m) through the mountain forests. Males and females look alike.

White band on hind wing

Metallic gold-green of male Silver Hairstreak

BICOLORED COMMODORE

HIGH FLIER
This iridescent butterfly reaches altitudes of between 5,900–9,840 ft (1,800–3,000 m) in the Himalayas. Its common name, Silver Hairstreak, comes from the silvery undersides of its wings. The caterpillars feed on oak leaves.

Tiny tail

ALPINE MEADOWS

GRASSY MEADOWS OCCUR above the tree line on mountain slopes. It is cold and windy and the soils are too thin for trees or bushes to survive. However, when the snows melt, an abundance of wildflowers and grasses attract butterflies and moths. Since summers are short, species tend to breed only once a year.

ROCK ROSE

ALPINE FLOWERS

During the brief summer, gentians, crocuses, and other beautiful flowers flourish on mountain slopes. The soils are well watered, since they are covered in snow for over half the year.

HIGH MOUNTAIN BLUE

Bluish gray wings of male

SLOW DEVELOPERS

The eggs of the High Mountain Blue may be found on rock-jasmine. The caterpilla feeds on alpine plants and develops more slowly than its lowland relatives.

Orange patches

Swollen, curved tip to antenna

Dark brown uppersides

ALPINE SKIPPER

ALPINE SKIPPER

This Skipper is found in the mountains of southeast Australia. The adults are on the wing in February and March, and often feed on yellow flowers of the daisy family.

CYNTHIA'S FRITILLARY

Cynthia's Fritillary flies swiftly when not feeding on meadow flowers. It lives only in the European Alps and the mountains of Bulgaria. Since there are many similar-looking Fritillary species, both females and males use their scented pheromones to identify and attract a mate.

CYNTHIA'S FRITILLARY

Yellow, black, and orange checkered wing markings

Network of veins outlined by darker scales

PEAK WHITE BUTTERFLY

CLOSE RELATIVES

The Peak White butterfly of Europe and Asia is closely related to the Western White found in the mountains of the US. It is well adapted to living at altitudes of over 6,000 ft (1,830 m) and can be found in sunny mountain habitats.

WARNING SIGNALS

This striking Ruby Tiger moth can be found in the mountains of Europe, Japan, Canada, and the US at altitudes of up to 9,840 ft (3,000 m). The red and black abdomen and red wings warn predators of its disgusting taste.

Translucent, brown-red forewings

RUBY TIGER MOTH

Red and black markings indicate internal poisons

MOUNTAIN AVENS

BLUES

SMALL, SWIFT-FLYING
Blues are able to cope
with mountain winds
and are a common sight
in alpine meadows.
The males, with their
glittering metallic colors,
are usually more
conspicuous than the
females, which often
have little or no blue
on their wings. The
caterpillars of some
species live in close
association with ants.

Deep blue
male

ALPINE ARGUS

Dark brown
female

COLOR CONTRAST
When the male Alpine Argus is ready
to mate, he uses his gleaming colors to
attract a female. Her dull colors
help to hide her from predators
until she has laid her eggs.

Blue upperside

FURRY BLUE

Dull
colors
of underside

UPPER AND UNDERSIDES
Patches of brown scent scales
give this species of butterfly
its furry appearance. When at
rest, Blues close their wings
to hide their brightly colored
uppersides. The undersides
are often marked with rows of
tiny spots and rings on a
pale background.

IDAS BLUE

The caterpillar of the Idas Blue butterfly spends the winter in the warmth and security of an ants' nest. The caterpillar secretes a sugary liquid that the ants drink. The caterpillar pupates inside the ants' nest, from which the young adult eventually emerges – crawling out into the open air to stretch its wings.

Brown margin

IDAS BLUE

COMMON BLUE

This butterfly is often seen flying on sunny hillsides. Its body is covered with long, hairlike scales that trap the sun's warmth and help the Common Blue survive sudden drops in temperature. It lives in both mountainous and lowland habitats in North Africa, Europe, and temperate Asia.

Long, hairlike scales

COMMON BLUE

IRIDESCENT COLORS

The Blues' metallic colors are produced by the way their wing scales reflect sunshine. Their wings do not contain any blue pigment. Female Sonoran Blues have more orange on their wings than the males. They can be found in mountain canyons, on cliffs, and on rocky slopes in California and northern Mexico.

Silvery pale sky blue

SONORAN BLUE

REFERENCE
SECTION

CLASSIFICATION

LIVING THINGS are classified into a series of categories according to the features that they have in common. Butterflies and moths, collectively called *Lepidoptera*, are a distinct group within the animal kingdom. The order of *Lepidoptera* is divided into 120–150 families, depending on the authority consulted. These families are subdivided into over 170,000 individual species.

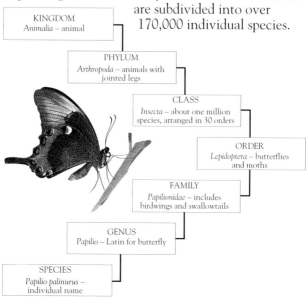

KINGDOM
Animalia – animal

PHYLUM
Arthropoda – animals with
jointed legs

CLASS
Insecta – about one million
species, arranged in 30 orders

ORDER
Lepidoptera – butterflies
and moths

FAMILY
Papilionidae – includes
birdwings and swallowtails

GENUS
Papilio – Latin for butterfly

SPECIES
Papilio palinurus –
individual name

FAMILY	EXAMPLES OF SPECIES	NOTES
MICROPTERIGIDAE	Pollen moths	Biting mouthparts in adults; mostly day fliers
INCURVARIIDAE	Long-horned moths, Yucca moths	Males of some species have very long antennae; Yucca moths are essential for pollination of yucca plants
HEPIALIDAE	Swift moths, Ghost moths	Wing-locking method differs from other moths; fore- and hindwings have similar shapes and vein patterns; most caterpillars bore into wood or roots
NEPTICULIDAE	Leaf-mining micromoths	Caterpillars tunnel between upper and lower surface of leaves; blotchy and snake-shaped mines can be seen on leaves
TINEIDAE	Clothes moths, Grain moths	Often dull-colored; feed on wool, furs, grains, and many products of economic importance
SESIIDAE	Hornet moths, Clearwings	Adults are camouflaged to look like bees or wasps but they cannot sting; most are day fliers and have stem-boring caterpillars
TORTRICIDAE	Apple Codling moths, Leaf-roller moths, Bell moths, Jumping Bean moths	Many species are pests of fruit, such as apple; caterpillar of Jumping Bean moth lives inside bean and causes it to "jump" when the caterpillar moves suddenly
PYRALIDAE	Pyralid moths	Includes a few aquatic moths; many pest species; Cactus moth used in biological control of prickly pear cactus in Australia
THYRIDIDAE	Leaf moths	The ragged outlines of many species' wings make them resemble leaves

Family	Examples of species	Notes
ZYGAENIDAE	Burnets, Forester moths	Brightly colored; mostly day-flying; often have well-developed tongues; many have highly toxic chemicals in their bodies to deter predators
ARCTIIDAE	Tiger moths, Footmen	Caterpillars often known as "Woolly Bears"; moths are often foul-tasting and brightly colored to deter predators
GEOMETRIDAE	Geometer moths, Looper moths	Huge family of worldwide moths; some species with wingless females; many pests; caterpillars have characteristic looping movement
SPHINGIDAE	Sphinx moths	Often large and powerful fliers; some species hover to feed at flowers; large caterpillars usually have a prominent (but not dangerous) horn at the rear
COSSIDAE	Goat moths, Carpenter moths	Many do not feed in the adult stage; caterpillars are generally wood-boring and commonly called Carpenter worms
ALUCITIDAE	Many-plumed moths	Small, delicate moths; subdued colors; feathery wings; each wing divided into six lobes; small, hairy caterpillars mine flower buds
LASIOCAMPIDAE	Eggar moths, Tent caterpillar moths, Lappet moths	Adults often have very fat, hairy abdomens; tongues often reduced and nonfunctional; several pest species
SATURNIIDAE	Giant silkmoths, Emperor moths	Some of the largest moths in the world; many have well-developed eyespots; males often have feathery antennae; proboscis often reduced; adults do not feed
BOMBYCIDAE	Silkmoths	A few wild species; "cultivated" silkmoth no longer exists in the wild; rounded, furry bodies; slightly hooked forewing tips; caterpillar produces silk

FAMILY	EXAMPLES OF SPECIES	NOTES
LYMANTRIIDAE	Tussock moths, Gypsy moths	Some species serious pests; usually hairy in appearance; dull-colored wings; lack functional tongue; do not feed as adults; females in many species cannot fly
URANIIDAE	Urania moths	Small family of moths including some resembling colorful butterflies; most are tropical; many have well-developed tails on wings
NOCTUIDAE	Owlets, Noctuids, Underwing moths	More than 20,000 species in this cosmopolitan family; caterpillars often attack roots; many are serious crop pests, including Armyworms and Cutworms
PTEROPHORIDAE	Plume moths	Small delicate moths; long-legged; narrow wings; forewings usually divided into two lobes, hindwing into three; at rest, often hold wings at right angles in "T" form
HESPERIIDAE	Skipper butterflies	Antennae often similar to moths; small but have large heads and stout bodies; fast-flying; caterpillars mostly feed on grass
PAPILIONIDAE	Swallowtails, Birdwing butterflies	Often have tails on hind wings; strong, gliding flight; many are tropical and brightly colored; often feed on plants poisonous to humans
PIERIDAE	Whites, Sulphurs, Yellow butterflies	Several pest species of whites have been accidentally spread around the world; many species are migratory
LYCAENIDAE	Blues, Hairstreaks, Copper butterflies	Family of over 5,000 butterflies; often brilliant metallic blue or copper; sexes often different colors; caterpillars of many species live in association with ants
NYMPHALIDAE	Emperors, Admirals, Fritillaries, Morpho butterflies	Over 5,000 species; forelegs reduced in size; many large and colorful species; many species migrate; commonly known as Brush-footed butterflies

AMAZING FACTS

THE LIFESTYLES and behavior of the 170,000 different species of butterflies and moths are almost as varied as the extraordinary colors and patterns that adorn their wings.

LIFE CYCLE

- .Goat moth caterpillars take 3–4 years to fully develop.
- The life cycle of the Indian Meal moth lasts only about four weeks.
- Cold-climate species can hibernate for as long as nine months.

EGGS

- Aquatic moths lay their eggs under water.
- Wax moths lay their eggs in beehives.
- *Danaine* females lay successive batches of eggs that are fertilized by different males.

CATERPILLARS

- The caterpillar of the Hawaiian moth *Eupithecia* catches flies.
- The Puss moth caterpillar spits acid when threatened.
- The caterpillar of the Io Moth has spines that sting like a nettle.
- Larger Orange Tip caterpillars eat the smaller caterpillars.
- Birdwings' caterpillars and chrysalids are eaten as delicacies in Papua New Guinea.
- The *Laetilia* caterpillar feeds on greenflies, rather than on plants.
- Large Blue caterpillars eat ant larvae.

PUPA

- The male Bagworm moth fertilizes the female while she is still in her cocoon.
- The pupa of the Striped Blue Crow is reflective and mirrors the colors around it.
- The Madagascan Saturniid has one of the largest cocoons, which is made of shiny silver silk.
- The color of the pupa of the Great Mormon butterfly changes to suit its background.
- Gold spots on the Queen butterfly pupa reflect light to distract predators.

ADULTS

• A hawkmoth from Madagascar has the longest proboscis – over 12 in (30 cm) long.

• Evening Brown butterflies usually fly at dusk and dawn.

• A migrating Monarch butterfly can fly 80 miles (130 km) per day.

• Patches of urine, full of mineral salts, attract butterflies in dry areas.

• The Zebra butterfly emits a foul smell to ward off predators.

• Male Long Horn moths have antennae up to six times the length of their bodies.

• Sphinx moths have sharp protective spines on their legs.

• In Japan, butterflies symbolize the souls of the dead.

• Vampire or Calpe moths from Southeast Asia can puncture skin and suck blood.

SHAPE AND SIZE

• Many-plumed moths have wings divided into six segments.

• Tails on the hind wings distract predators.

• The wing tips of the Giant Silkmoth look like snakes' heads.

• Ctenuchid moths resemble the shape of inedible Lycid beetles.

• The female Queen Alexandra's Birdwing is the largest butterfly – it has a 6–11 in (15–28 cm) wingspan.

• The *Thysania agrippina* moth has the largest wingspan: 9–12 in (23–30 cm).

• One of the smallest butterlies is the Grass Jewel with a ⅜ in–⅝-in (1–1.5-cm) wingspan.

• Nepticulid moths are the smallest moths – ⅛ in (0.3 cm) wingspan.

• The Atlas moth is the largest moth in the world.

PESTS

• Armyworm caterpillars may destroy hundreds of hectares of crops.

• The *Filodes* moth feeds on moisture around the eyes of cattle and can spread diseases

• In its lifetime, a single Black Arches moth caterpillar can eat about 1,000 pine needles and damage as many again.

• Wax moth caterpillars feed on beeswax and badly damage beehives.

FRIENDS

• 40,000 Silkmoth cocoons could provide enough silk to encircle the earth at the Equator with a single thread.

• In Australia, the voracious Cactus Moth has helped farmers to clear large areas of land of prickly pear cacti.

HABITATS UNDER THREAT

BEFORE HUMAN LIFE flourished on Earth, habitats and animal and plant species were destroyed purely by climatic changes or natural disasters such as volcanic eruptions. However, people have increased the pressures on the natural world, causing pollution and using land for agriculture, timber, mining, and building projects. Moths and butterflies living in affected habitats are among the first species to suffer.

HABITAT	THREATS	SPECIES AT RISK
Rain forests	Rain forests, particulary rich in *Lepidoptera*, are under threat from logging for timber, clearing and draining farmland, and mining.	The Esmeralda, Brazilian Dynastor, Blue Morpho, Australian Atlas moth, Queen Alexandra's Birdwing
Tropical dry forests	Less common than rain forests, tropical dry forests are threatened by fires and clearance for farming. Countries such as Costa Rica have made efforts to preserve these special habitats.	Tiger Pierid, Leaf Moth, Macrogonia Moth
Temperate forests	Many areas have been cleared for agriculture or replaced by coniferous forests. Some areas have been affected by acid rain and by polluted water drained off from nearby farmland. A rich source of timber for industry and furniture.	Purple Emperor, Silver-washed Fritillary, Pearly Eye, Black Hairstreak

Habitat	Threats	Species at Risk
Mountains	Overgrazing on the lower slopes and increased use of the higher slopes for skiing and other winter vacation resorts put many mountain habitats at risk.	Apollo, Checkerspot, Alpine Erebias, Gavarnie Blue, Mountain Small White, Corsican Swallowtail, Long-tailed Beauty moth
Wetlands	There are few places in the world where wetlands are not under some threat. Drainage usually provides fertile farmland or land may be used for forestry. In some areas, peat extraction on a commercial scale is a serious threat.	Marsh Fritillary, Bog Copper, Large Copper, Mitchell's Satyr, Bog Fritillary, Mulberry Wing butterfly, False Ringlet
Pastures	Traditional pastures are often enriched with fertilizers to enhance feed available for grazing livestock. Aggressive species of plants take over and this reduces the diversity of other plants and, in turn, the variety of *Lepidoptera*.	Small Blue, Scarce Copper, Tessellated Skipper, Beardgrass Skipper, Eltham Skipper
Grasslands	Grasslands are now often seeded with "improved" types of grass, which make better animal feed but attract fewer species of butterfly. Grasslands are also under intense pressure for housing and other building development.	Southern Skipperling, Large Blue, Twin Spot Fritillary, Meadow Fritillary
Nature reserves	In order to maintain balance, nature reserves must be managed. Long and short grasses support different species of butterflies and moths. By removing "undesirable" invasive plants, the species that feed on them also disappear.	Species affected depend on management plan; what may be good for one species may be bad for another

OBSERVING

BUTTERFLIES AND MOTHS can be disturbed by the slightest movement, so you will need plenty of patience to get near enough to study them. Probably the best time to observe them is when they are eating and drinking. In time, you will soon discover the best sites.

WATCHING CODE

- Do not kill species in order to identify them.
- Examine them in a glass tube or pill box; release them unharmed.
- Some countries do not allow collecting or the use of nets.
- Certain species are legally protected.
- Take care not to damage the habitat or trample on crops.

NOTEBOOK AND FIELD GUIDE

YOU WILL NEED

CAMERA

SHORT-FOCUS TELESCOPE

PILL BOXES

RECORDING YOUR OBSERVATIONS

Keep a notebook to make quick sketches and record observations on where and when the insect was found, its behavior, appearance, and habitat. A short-focus telescope will reveal details barely visible to the naked eye and a field guide will help you check your identification of the species. Take a camera along; photographs are useful for further study.

WHERE TO LOOK

EGG-LAYING SITES
These sites need to be
protected; look on
the hidden undersides
of leaves and near buds.

CATERPILLAR FOOD PLANTS
Look for caterpillars
feeding on leaves and
blades of grass. Many
larvae are camouflaged.

SHELTERED SPOTS
Butterflies bask in the
sun, sheltered from wind.
Many species lay their
eggs in sheltered spots.

FEEDING STATIONS
Flowers are the best food
supply; butterflies and
moths are attracted by
their color and scent.

HEDGEROWS
Many butterflies and
moths can be found on
plants, sheltered
underneath shrubs.

DAMP GROUND
In hot climates, moths
and butterflies drink
from the damp ground
in forests.

LIQUID SOURCES
Butterflies and moths
can be found feeding on
juicy, overripe fruit or
drinking from puddles.

OOZING SAP
Moths and butterflies
gorge on sap oozing from
trees. At night, use a
flashlight to see moths.

LIGHT
Moths fly toward light at
night; look for them on
store windows and
streetlights.

REARING

ONE OF THE BEST ways to
study moths and butterflies
is to rear them from eggs.
Many species can be bred
in captivity. Remember to
find out which plants the
caterpillars eat before the
eggs hatch.

PEACOCK
BUTTERFLY

CHOSEN SPECIES
It takes a couple of months to rear a
Peacock butterfly from egg to adult.

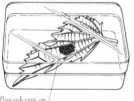

Peacock eggs on
food plant

1 Place eggs laid by a captive female (or
eggs found on nettles in the field) in a
small plastic box. Keep the box closed to
ensure that the leaves do not dry out.
When they hatch, transfer the small
caterpillars to a larger container.

Small caterpillars
like young nettle
leaves

Lift
caterpillar
gently

2 Handle the caterpillars as little as
possible. Use a fine paintbrush to
transfer a caterpillar from one container
to another.

3 Place leaves of the caterpillars' food
plant in a clear plastic container. To
absorb excess moisture, place absorbent
paper in the bottom or replace the
container's lid with gauze. Feed the
caterpillars regularly with fresh leaves.

4 Transfer the caterpillars to a larger container as they grow larger. Put fresh cuttings from the caterpillars' food plant in a cage made of netting, or inside a clear plastic container with a perforated lid to provide adequate light and ventilation. The food must be inspected regularly and replaced when necessary.

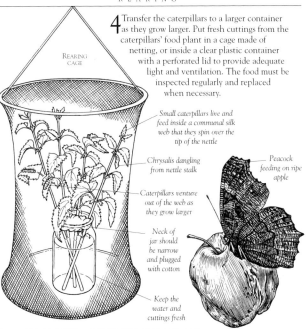

REARING CAGE

Small caterpillars live and feed inside a communal silk web that they spin over the tip of the nettle

Chrysalis dangling from nettle stalk

Caterpillars venture out of the web as they grow larger

Neck of jar should be narrow and plugged with cotton

Keep the water and cuttings fresh

Peacock feeding on ripe apple

WARNING BOX

• It is illegal to release nonnative species into the wild.

• Releasing captive species can upset mating patterns among the local wild population.

• Consult a conservation group before releasing captive-bred species.

• If large numbers are released, you could create competition if food is scarce.

5 Keep the adult female butterfly for a short period to obtain eggs. Feed her on a weak sugar solution, cut flowers, or very ripe fruit. Release the butterfly if it is a species native to your country.

BUTTERFLY GARDEN

NECTAR-BEARING PLANTS attract moths and butterflies
to gardens all over the world. To provide a continuous
food supply, grow a range of plants that bloom at
different times of the year. If you grow plants that the
caterpillars can eat, the insects
may breed in your garden.

RED ADMIRAL

BLUE TRIANGLE

Red band

Powerful flier

Elongated
forewing

Veins cut
across
turquoise
bands

BLUE TRIANGLE
This colorful butterfly is frequently
seen in Australian gardens and is
widespread throughout Asia. It feeds
on many garden plants, such as
buddleia, hebe, lantana, and verbena.

SUMMER BUTTERFLIES
Throughout Europe, Asia, the
US, Canada, and Hawaii, the
Red Admiral is quite
common on all garden
plants, especially after
a long, warm
summer. The
caterpillars
often feed on
nettles in
semishaded
areas.

HEBE

BUDDLEIA

SILVER-STRIPED HAWKMOTH

Pink base to hind wing

NECTAR

Hawkmoths use their long proboscis to suck nectar from the deep tubular florets of honeysuckle. Hovering over flowers, Silver-Striped Hawkmoths visit gardens across Europe, Africa, and Australasia.

Night-scented flowers, such as honeysuckle, attract moths

Clouded Yellow butterflies feed on clovers, rich in nectar

WILD GARDEN

If you leave a small part of the garden to grow wild, you will attract a wider variety of species. Many females lay their eggs on wild grasses and nettles, the food plants of many caterpillars.

Moths and butterflies like strongly scented flowers

LAVENDER

Large wings

MONARCH

Monarchs visit gardens in cold climates but need warmth to breed

GARDEN VISITORS

As Monarchs migrate across North America, they visit garden flowers to "fuel up" for their journey and the winter. Less frequently, they can be spotted in gardens in Europe and Australasia. Monarchs have been recorded feeding on more than 24 varieties of wild and cultivated plants.

Resources

These are just some of the centers around the world where you can obtain further information about moths and butterflies.

COLLECTIONS

AUSTRALIA

Australian National Insect Collection
Care of CSIRO Division of Entomology
P.O. Box 1700
Canberra, ACT 2601

BRAZIL

Wildlife Museum
São Cristónão
Rio de Janeiro

CANADA

National Museum of Natural Sciences
Metcalfe & McLeod Sts.
Ottowa, Ontario

FRANCE

Musée National d'Histoire Naturelle
Jardin des Plantes
Rue Cuvier, Paris 75005

GERMANY

Museum für Naturkunde der Homboldt-Universität zu Berlin
Invalidenstrasse
Berlin 1040

JAPAN

Osaka Museum of Natural History
Higashisumiyoshi-ku
Osaka

MALAYSIA

National Museum of Malaysia
Damansara
Kuala Lumur

SOUTH AFRICA

South African Museum
P.O. Box 61
Cape Town 9000

SPAIN

Museo Nacional de Ciencias Naturales
José Gutiérrez Abascal
28006 Madrid

SWEDEN

Swedish Museum of Natural History
P.O. Box 50007
S-104 05 Stockholm

UNITED KINGDOM

Natural History Museum
Cromwell Road
London SW7 5BD

UNITED STATES

There are many; here are six of the largest in the US:
Allyn Museum of Entomology
3621 Bay Shore Rd.
Sarasota, FL 34234

American Museum of Natural History
Central Park West
at 79th St.
New York, NY 10024

Bishop Museum
P.O. Box 19000–A
Honolulu, HI 96817

**Carnegie Museum
of Natural History**
4400 Forbes Ave.
Pittsburgh, PA 15213

**Denver Museum
of Natural History**
2001 Colorado Blvd.
Denver, CO 80205

**National Museum
of Natural History**
Smithsonian Institution
Washington, DC 20560

CONSERVATION SOCIETIES
*Specializing in insect
conservation.*

UNITED KINGDOM
**The Butterfly
Conservation Society**
P.O. Box 222
Dedham, Essex C07 6DE

World Wildlife Fund
Panda House
Weyside Park
Godalming, Surrey

UNITED STATES
**National Audubon
Society**
700 Broadway
New York, NY 10003

The Xerxes Society
10 SW Ash St.
Portland, OR 97204

BUTTERFLY GARDENS
*There are many local
butterfly farms – larger
wildlife organizations can
give more information*

UNITED KINGDOM
London Zoo
Regents Park
London NW1 4RY

**Worldwide Butterflies
and Lullington Silk Farm**
Crompton House
Nr. Sherbourne
Dorset DT9 4QN

UNITED STATES
*There are over 100 in the
US.; these are two of the
best-known*

Butterfly World
Tradewinds Park
3600 West Sample Rd.
Coconut Creek, FL 33073

**The Day Butterfly
Center**
Callaway Gardens
Pine Mountain,
GA 31822

INSECT SOCIETIES

INTERNATIONAL
*Largest and best-known
international organization
for amateurs and
professionals interested in
the study of Lepidoptera
(butterflies and moths)*

**The Lepidopterists'
Society**
c/o Julian, P. Donahue,
Assistant Secretary
Natural History Museum
of Los Angeles County
900 Exposition Blvd.
Los Angeles, CA 90007

BOOKS AND EQUIPMENT
*Best supply source for
entomological books and
equipment in the US*

Bioquip Products
17803 LaSalle Ave.
Gardena, CA 90248

Glossary

ABDOMEN
Segmented rear part of
the body behind the
thorax. It contains
the digestive and
reproductive organs.

ANDROCONIA
Special scent scales,
found in male butterflies,
that disperse pheromones.
See PHEROMONES.

ANTENNAE
Sensory organs on the
heads of adults and
caterpillars. They are
mainly used for smelling
and touching.

BROADLEAF
Having wide leaves
(deciduous trees).

CAMOUFLAGE
To disguise the body
with colors, markings,
or patterns that blend
with the surroundings.

CHRYSALIS
Butterfly pupa. See PUPA.

CLASPERS
Two pincers on the end
of the abdomen; the male
uses them to grasp the
female while mating.

COCOON
A protective silk case,
which some caterpillars

weave around their
bodies before pupating.

COLONY
A community of
individuals of the same
species that live together.

COMPOUND EYE
An eye consisting of
many light-sensitive units
called ommatidia.

DIGESTION
The process by which
food is broken down and
absorbed into the body.

ECDYSIS
The molting process by
which the caterpillar
changes its skin as it
grows larger.

ESTIVATE
To remain dormant
during heat or drought
in order to survive.

EXOSKELETON
The hard, external
covering of the body.

EYESPOTS
Circular markings on the
wings that look like
eyes to deter predators.

FERTILIZATION
The union of a male
sex cell and a female sex
cell during the
reproduction process.

HIBERNATION
The resting state in
which butterflies and
moths pass the winter in
temperate regions. All
the body processes slow
down to conserve energy.

HONEYDEW
A sweet, sticky liquid
excreted by aphids,
which comes from the
sap of the plants on
which they feed.

IRIDESCENT
Bright rainbowlike
coloring that shimmers
and changes constantly.

LARVA
The wingless, immature
form, which is also
known as a caterpillar.

LEPIDOPTERA
The order of insects to
which butterflies and
moths belong.

MANDIBLE
One of a pair of jawlike
mouthparts used to bite
or chew food.

METAMORPHOSIS
The series of changes
in body structure that
occurs during the
growing process of
moths and butterflies.

Moths and butterflies undergo complete metamorphosis, which comprises four distinct phases – egg, caterpillar, pupa, and adult stage.

MIGRATION
Flight to a new area, often prompted by seasonal or climatic change or the need for fresh food supplies.

MIMICRY
The process whereby one species of butterfly or moth copies the appearance and behavior of another species to gain protection from predators.

NECTAR
A sugary fluid produced by plants that encourages butterflies and moths to visit and pollinate flowers.

NOCTURNAL
To be active at night and to rest during the day.

OCELLI
Simple eyes that respond mainly to light and shade.

OMMATIDIUM
A single facet of a compound eye.

OVERWINTER
See HIBERNATION.

PALPS
Taste organs beside the mouthparts on the head.

PHEROMONES
Scented chemical substances released by butterflies and moths of both sexes to signal that they are ready to mate.

PIGMENT
A colored substance that occurs in plant and animal tissues.

POLLEN
A dustlike powder in flowers that contains the male sex cells.

POLLINATION
The transfer of pollen from the male parts to the female parts of flowers or cones so that seeds can develop.

PROBOSCIS
Elongated mouthparts that usually act as a feeding tube.

PROLEGS
Suckerlike structures along the caterpillar's abdomen that lack joints but function as legs.

PUPA, PUPAL STAGE
The inactive, nonfeeding stage in the life cycle during which the caterpillar is transformed into an adult.

SCALES
Flattened, platelike hairs that cover moths and butterflies.

SPECIES
A group of animals or plants that can breed only with each other to produce fertile offspring.

SPINNERET
Organ in caterpillars through which silk, secreted by the silk gland, is spun into threads and pushed out into the air to form webs and cocoons.

SPIRACLES
External openings of the breathing tubes, located on the sides of the body.

THORAX
Middle part of the body, between the head and the abdomen.

ULTRAVIOLET
Light beyond the violet end of the color spectrum, invisible to the human eye but visible to insects.

WARNING COLORS
Bold, conspicuous colors to warn predators that a butterfly or moth is poisonous.

WINGSPAN
Measurement from one wing tip to the other.

Common and scientific names

Adonis Blue
Lysandra bellargus
African Grass Blue
Zizeeria knysna
African Leaf Butterfly
Kallimoides rumia
African Moon Moth
Argema mimosae
African Ringlet
Ypthima asterope
Alpine Argus
Albulina orbitulus
Alpine Skipper
Oreisplanus munionga
Antler Moth
Cerapteryx graminis
Arctic Fritillary
Clossiana chariclea
Atlas moth
Attacus atlas

Banksia Moth
Danima banksiae
Bent-wing Ghost moth
Zelotypia stacyi
Bhutan Glory
Bhutanitis lidderdalei
Bicolor Commodore
Limenitis zayla
Black-and-white Tiger
Danaus affinis
Black Arches
Lymantria monacha
Black-veined White
Aporia crataegi

Blue Pansy
Junonia orithya
Blue Tharops
Menander menander
Blue Triangle
Graphium sarpedon
Bogong Moth
Agrotis infusa
Brazilian Morpho
Morpho aega
Brazilian Skipper
Calpodes ethlius
Brimstone Moth
Opisthograptis luteolata
Brindled Beauty
Lycia hirtaria
Brown China-mark
Elophila nympheata
Brown Hooded Owlet
Cucullia convexipennis
Buckeye
Junonia coenia
Butler's Brahmin
Dactylocerus swanzii

Cairns Birdwing
Ornithoptera priamus
California Dog-face
Zerene eurydice
Cardinal Fritillary
Pandoriana pandora
Cinnabar Moth
Tyria jacobeae
Citrus Swallowtail
Papilio demodocus

Cleopatra
Gonepteryx cleopatra
Clouded Yellow
Colias croceus
Cloudless Giant
Sulphur
Phoebis sennae
Comma
Polygonia c-album
Common Blue
Polyommatus icarus
Common Brown
Heteronympha merope
Common Clothes Moth
Tineola bisselliella
Common Eggfly
Hypolimnas bolina
Common Emperor
Bunaea alcinoe
Common Glider
Neptis sappho
Common Imperial Blue
Jalmenus evagoras
Common Mormon
Papilio polytes
Common Opal
Poecilmitis thysbe
Cramer's Blue Morpho
Morpho rhetenor
Crimson Speckled Moth
Utetheisa pulchella
Crimson Tip
Colotis danae
Cruiser Butterfly
Vindula erota

Cynthia's Fritillary
Euphydryas cynthia

Dark Chopper
Gonometa postica
Dark Green Fritillary
Argynnis aglaja
Death's Head
Hawkmoth
Acherontia atropos
Dingy Skipper
Erynnis tages
Diva Moth
Divana diva
Doherty's Longtail
Himantopterus dohertyi
Dotted Checkerspot
Poladryas minuta
Drinker Moth
Philudoria potatoria
Dryad Butterfly
Minois dryas
Duke of Burgundy
Hamearis lucina

Eastern Flat Skipper
Netrocoryne repanda
Elephant Hawkmoth
Deilephila elpenor
Emperor Gum Moth
Opodiphthera eucalypti
Esmeralda Butterfly
Cithaerias esmeralda
Evening Brown
Melanitis leda

False Clothes Moth
Hofmannophila

pseudospretella
Fiery Campylotes
Campylotes desgodinsi
Forester
Adscita statices
Foxy Charaxes
Charaxes jasius
Freak Butterfly
Calinaga buddha
Furry Blue
Agrodiaetus dolus

Garden Tiger
Arctia caja
Ghost Moth
Hepialus humuli
Giant African Skipper
Pyrrhochalcia iphis
Giant Agrippa
Thysania agrippina
Giant Anthelid
Chelepteryx collesi
Glasswing
Acraea andromacha
Goat Moth
Cossus cossus
Golden Clearwing
Albuna oberthuri
Grass Jewel
Freyeria trochylus
Great Oak Beauty
Boarmia roboraria
Great Orange Tip
Hebomoia glaucippe
Grizzled Skipper
Pyrgus malvae
Guineafowl Butterfly
Hamanumidia daedalus

Gypsy Moth
Lymantria dispar

Harvester
Feniseca tarquinius
Heath Fritillary
Mellicta athalia
Herald
Scoliopteryx libatrix
Hercules Moth
Coscinocera hercules
Hermit
Chazara briseis
Hewitson's Blue
Hairstreak
Thecla coronata
High Mountain Blue
Agriades franklinii
Holly Blue
Celastrina argiolus
Hornet Moth
Sesia apiformis
Hummingbird
Hawkmoth
*Macroglossum
stellatarum*

Idas Blue
Lycaeides idas
Indian Leaf Butterfly
Kallima inachus
Indian Moon Moth
Actias selene
Io Moth
Automeris io

Japanese Swallowtail
Papilio xuthus

Jersey Tiger
Euplagia quadripunctaria

King's Bee Hawkmoth
Cephonodes kingi

Lang's Short-tailed Blue
Syntarucus pirithous
Large Blue
Maculinea arion
Large Blue Charaxes
Charaxes bohemani
Large Checkered Skipper
Heteropterus morpheus
Large Copper
Lycaena dispar
Large Heath
Coenonympha tullia
Large Skipper
Ochlodes venatus
Large Tortoiseshell
Nymphalis polychloros
Large Tree Nymph
Idea leuconoe
Large White
Pieris brassicae
Leopard Moth
Zeuzera pyrina
Little Tiger Blue
Tarucus balkanicus
Lobster Moth
Stauropus fagi
Long-tailed Skipper
Urbanus proteus

Madagascan Sunset Moth
Chrysiridia riphearia
Magpie Moth
Abraxas grossulariata

Malay Lacewing
Cethosia hypsaea
Many-plumed Moth
Orneodes dohertyi
Marbled White
Melanargia galathea
Marsh Fritillary
Eurodryas aurinia
Meadow Brown
Maniola jurtina
Monarch
Danaus plexippus
Moorland Clouded
Yellow
Colias palaeno
Mother-of-pearl Morpho
Morpho laertes
Mourning Cloak
Nymphalis antiopa

Northern Clouded Yellow
Colias hecla

Oaksilk Moth
Antheraea harti
Old Lady Moth
Mormo maura
Oleander Hawkmoth
Daphnis nerii
Orange Albatross
Appias nero
Orange Sulphur
Colias eurytheme
Orange Tip
Anthocharis cardamines
Orizaba Silkmoth
Rothschildia orizaba
Owl Butterfly
Caligo idomeneus

Owl Moth
Brahmaea wallichii

Painted Lady
Cynthia cardui
Palla Butterfly
Palla ussheri
Palm Skipper
Zophopetes dysmephila
Passion-vine Butterfly
Heliconius ismenius
Peacock
Inachis io
Peak White Butterfly
Pontia callidice
Peppered Moth
Biston betularia
Piedmont Ringlet
Erebia meolans
Pine Emperor Moth
Nudaurelia cytherea
Pine Processionary
*Thaumetopoea
pityocampa*
Pine-tree Lappet
Dendrolimus pini
Pine White
Neophasia menapia
Pink-barred Sallow
Xanthia togata
Pirate Butterfly
Catacroptera cloanthe
Poplar Hawkmoth
Laothoe populi
Postman Butterfly
Heliconius melpomene
Purple-edged Copper
*Palaeochrysophanus
hippothoe*

Purple Hairstreak
  Quercusia quercus
Puss Moth
  Cerura vinula

Queen Alexandra's
  Birdwing
  Ornithoptera alexandrae
Queen Butterfly
  Danaus gilippus
Queen Cracker
  Hamadryas arethusa

Rajah Brooke's Birdwing
  Troides brookiana
Red Underwing
  Catocala nupta
Regent Skipper
  Euschemon rafflesia
Ringlet
  Aphantopus hyperantus
Robin Moth
  Hyalophora cecropia
Royal Walnut Moth
  Citheronia regalis
Ruby Tiger
  Phragmatobia fuliginosa

Scarlet Tiger
  Callimorpha dominula
Schulze's Agrias
  Agrias claudia
Silkmoth
  Bombyx mori
Silver Butterfly
  Argyrophorus argenteus
Silver Hairstreak
  Chrysozephyrus syla
Silver-spotted Skipper
  Hesperia comma

Silver-striped Hawkmoth
  Hippotion celerio
Silver-studded Blue
  Plebejus argus
Silver-washed Fritillary
  Argynnis paphia
Small Copper
  Lycaena phlaeas
Smaller Wood Nymph
  Ideopsis gaura
Small Postman
  Heliconius erato
Small Tortoiseshell
  Aglais urticae
Small White
  Pieris rapae
Sonoran Blue
  Philotes sonorensis
Spanish Festoon
  Zerynthia rumina
Spanish Moon Moth
  Graellsia isabellae
Speckled Wood
  Pararge aegeria
Splendid Ghost Moth
  Aenetus mirabilis
Striped Blue Crow
  Euploea mulciber
Striped Hawkmoth
  Hyles lineata
Swallowtail
  Papilio machaon
Swamp Metalmark
  Calephelis mutica

Tawny Rajah
  Charaxes bernardus
Tiger Pierid
  Dismorphia amphione

Tiger Swallowtail
  Papilio glaucus
Two-tailed Pasha
  Charaxes jasius

Vampire Moth
  Calyptra eustrigata
Variable Burnet Moth
  Zygaena ephialtes
Verdant Sphinx
  Euchloron megaera
Viceroy
  Basilarchia archippus

Wall Brown
  Lasiommata megera
Water Tiger
  Paracles laboulbeni
White Admiral
  Ladoga camilla
White Ermine
  Spilosoma lubricipeda
White Peacock
  Anartia jatrophae
Woodland Grayling
  Hipparchia fagi
Wood White
  Leptidea sinapis

Yellow Coster
  Acraea vesta
Yellow-spot Blue
  Candalides xanthospilos
Yucca Giant Skipper
  Megathymus yuccae

Zebra Butterfly
  Colobura dirce
Zebra Swallowtail
  Eurytides marcellus

Index